Advance praise for

Ornament of Dakpo Kagyü Thought

"Everybody in the Kagyü lineage knows the pithy and touching verses of the third Karmapa's famous *Aspiration Prayer of Mahāmudrā*, which are like the well-shaped limbs of a beautiful body. Their being adorned by Mendong Tsampa's concise *Ornament* skillfully elicits just the right amount of thoughts to shine a light on thought-free mahāmudrā. In the mirror of Sarah Harding's fine introduction and translation, we are now enabled to clearly see all these adornments pointing back at naked mahāmudrā in its unadorned state."

—Karl Brunnhölzl, author of *Milarepa's Kungfu: Mahāmudrā in His Songs of Realization*

"I well remember, durin ed
with Sarah this delightf a-
pa's *Mahāmudrā Aspira* fit
I derived at that time from reading Mendong Tsampa's words are mirrored now by the pleasure of knowing that Sarah has brought this gem into English for others to benefit."

—Richard Barron (Chökyi Nyima), translator of *The Autobiography of Jamgön Kongtrul: A Gem of Many Colors*

"Sarah Harding clarifies the essence of mahāmudrā with characteristic humor and penetrating insight, including points of contention. These pithy texts, elegantly translated, are contemplations on lucid awareness and immeasurable compassion, sparking illumination while refreshing one's language skills!"

—Karma Lekshe Tsomo, professor of Buddhist Studies, University of San Diego

"Mendong Tsampa's commentary on the third Karmapa's famous *Mahāmudrā Aspiration Prayer* is a perfect balance of depth and concision, and Sarah Harding's presentation—from her introduction to her translation and notes—also strikes the perfect balance of precision and readability. *Ornament of Dakpo Kagyü Thought* opens up the profundity and brilliance of the *Mahāmudrā Aspiration Prayer* in a direct and lucid way—it's the middle-length commentary we've all needed! This book will be savored by all who are inspired by the path of mahāmudrā, from those starting out to seasoned Buddhist practitioners and scholars."

—Elizabeth Callahan, translator of *Moonbeams of Mahāmudrā*

Ornament of Dakpo Kagyü Thought

SHORT COMMENTARY ON THE
Mahāmudrā Aspiration Prayer

BY MENDONG TSAMPA,
KARMA NGEDÖN TENGYÉ

Translated, introduced, and annotated
by Sarah Harding

Wisdom Publications
199 Elm Street
Somerville, MA 02144 USA
wisdomexperience.org

© 2022 Sarah Harding
All rights reserved.

No part of this book may be reproduced in any form or by any means, electronic or mechanical, including photography, recording, or by any information storage and retrieval system or technologies now known or later developed, without permission in writing from the publisher.

Library of Congress Cataloging-in-Publication Data
Names: Karma-nges-don-bstan-rgyas, active 1891, author. | Harding, Sarah, 1951– translator.
Title: Ornament of Dakpo Kagyü thought: short commentary on the Mahāmudrā aspiration prayer / by Mendong Tsampa Karma Ngedön Tengyé; translated, introduced, and annotated by Sarah Harding.
Description: First edition. | Somerville: Wisdom Publications, 2022. | Includes bibliographical references and index.
Identifiers: LCCN 2021056664 (print) | LCCN 2021056665 (ebook) | ISBN 9781614297185 (paperback) | ISBN 9781614297314 (ebook)
Subjects: LCSH: Mahāmudrā (Tantric rite). | Bka'-brgyud-pa (Sect)—Rituals. | Buddhist poetry, Tibetan—History and criticism.
Classification: LCC BQ8921.M35 K36 2022 (print) | LCC BQ8921.M35 (ebook) | DDC 294.3/4435—dc23/eng/20220202
LC record available at https://lccn.loc.gov/2021056664
LC ebook record available at https://lccn.loc.gov/2021056665

ISBN 978-1-61429-718-5 ebook ISBN 978-1-61429-731-4

26 25 24 23 22 5 4 3 2 1

Cover design by Gopa & Ted 2. Interior design by Tony Lulek.
Cover image: An ancient seal of the Karmapas, used with permission of His Holiness Ogyen Trinley Dorje, the Seventeenth Karmapa.

Printed on acid-free paper that meets the guidelines for permanence and durability of the Production Guidelines for Book Longevity of the Council on Library Resources.

Printed in the United States of America.

Please visit fscus.org.

Contents

Preface vi

Introduction 1

Aspiration Prayer of Definitive Mahāmudrā 15
by Karmapa Rangjung Dorjé

Short Commentary on the
Mahāmudrā Aspiration Prayer 21
by Mendong Tsampa Rinpoché

Notes 103

Bibliography 111

Index 121

About the Translator 131

Preface

The *Aspiration Prayer of Definitive Mahāmudrā* by Lord Rangjung Dorjé has long been my favorite prayer, ever since its daily recitation as part of the curriculum in the three-year retreat. It seems to just roll off the tongue (in Tibetan, that is), yet without losing transparency of meaning like many other lightning-fast recitations. I have used many of its verses in Tibetan classes over the years, particularly for exercises in memorization, as well as translation. In the two-week summer Tibetan Intensive of 2018, sponsored by the Tsadra Foundation and held at the University of Colorado Boulder, I decided to use this lovely and accessible commentary by Mendong Tsampa Rinpoché as the study topic for the advanced track in classical Tibetan. It was a remarkable experience to work on this as a group, and an intelligent group at that. I am used to working alone, but this was a very enriching process for me, and hopefully for the students as well. There was so much interchange of ideas and words and research, I really regard it as an international committee translation project, although admittedly I had the last say in this final translation submitted to Wisdom Publications. I would therefore like to mention and thank all of the students. I am sure many of them will go on to be well-known scholar-practitioners (if they are not already).

Alina Cepeda
Ralph H. Craig III
Allan Yi Ding
Renée Ford
Tucker Foley
Benjamin Goldstein
Cheryl Lins
Aaron McNeil
Katrin Querl

Our support team from the Tsadra Foundation, Marcus Perman and the staff, facilitated the ease of learning, and our ever-helpful Tibetan informant, Ācārya Lama Tenpa Gyaltsen, clarified difficult points. Many of these students were also in Jules Levinson's advanced colloquial class, where they listened to tapes of Khenchen Thrangu Rinpoché's teachings on the same prayer, which must now be indelibly etched in their minds forever, as it is in mine. Of course we could not finish the whole translation in two weeks, but I kept plugging away at it to the end with two hardy and highly motivated students: Tucker Foley and Ben Goldstein.

And so I present this final product in the hopes that ever more students and their teachers will find it useful—for inspiration, for studying Tibetan, for the awakening of the world.

Sarah Harding
Boulder, Colorado
August 2021

Introduction

The *Mahāmudrā Aspiration Prayer* by the Third Karmapa Rangjung Dorjé (1284–1339) is certainly one of the most brilliant and popular compositions we have on mahāmudrā. What seems to be a heartfelt prayer in twenty-five quatrains of easygoing nine-meter verse that lends itself to chanting and ritualized group prayer is at the same time intricately organized into the most profound and thorough exposition of the practice and theory of mahāmudrā, the pinnacle of practice in the Kagyü school of Buddhism in Tibet. Because of that, it is widely used even now, some seven centuries later, both as a deep contemplative practice and as a springboard for far-ranging Dharma talks.

The earliest written commentary appeared about four centuries later (in 1733), composed by the great lineage holder Situ Paṇchen Chökyi Jungné, Tenpai Nyinjé (1700–1774). *The Oral Transmission of the Supreme Siddhas*, though described by its author as "brief," is a good example of how the great masters and erudites of Tibet could expand a short prayer into an encyclopedia of Buddhist thought. A lot to handle for the average meditator. Mendong Tsampa Rinpoché (1867–1921?), exercising kindness to the reader, composed this *Ornament of Dakpo Kagyü Thought*, reducing it by about one-third. His contemporary, Karma Rinchen Dargyé (ca. 1835–ca. 1917),

made an even shorter version.[1] But as Goldilocks discovered, the middle way is perfect.

Mahāmudrā

Mahāmudrā as we know it is a name for the practice and culminating realization of nondual suchness in several lineages of Tibetan Buddhism, especially in the Kagyü. However, the term itself, as well as the practice, had a long and somewhat complicated history along a bumpy road before it arrived at this pristine state. The simplest level of complication is twofold: that it means one thing in a tantric context and another in relation to sutra or the path of the perfections. But even in that there is much to unpack. Fortunately for us, and especially for someone writing a bare-bones introduction, there are now many studies and publications to do that.

In Sanskrit, *mahā* means "great" or "big," and that's where the simplicity ends. The root meaning of the term *mudrā* is "seal," and by extension the imprints left by a seal, like signs or symbols.[2] In Indian literature it further indicates a ritual hand gesture or pose (from the Indian traditions of dance), a yogic posture, and the consort of a male practitioner or deity. In connection with the first meaning, we often see the English translation "great seal" with concordant explanations. The Tibetan translators added an honorific "hand" (*phyag*) to seal (*rgya*), making "chakgya chenpo" (*phyag rgya chen po*). Although there is no "hand" in the Sanskrit, that didn't stop Tibetan commentators from engaging in one of their favorite scholarly activities, often called "creative etymology." For example:

> *Hand* is the timeless awareness of emptiness.
> *Seal* means that there is nothing beyond that.
> *Great* means there is nothing higher than that.[3]

Traditionally mahāmudrā is described as that which seals all phenomena, like a sovereign's sealed edict, such that once that true nature is realized, there is nothing to which it does not apply—it is the law of the land. Here is a similar example from Situ Tenpai Nyinjé's commentary:

> The essence of mahāmudrā is untransgressable (*mi 'da'*), so mahāmudrā is called a "seal" (*mudrā*; *phyag rgya*). For example, just as local ministers, governors, and so on cannot transgress the command that has the seal of authority of a great universal sovereign, in the same way, the variety of inner and outer phenomena do not transgress the essence of unified spontaneous timeless awareness. That is why it is a seal. *Mahā* means it is great, because it is the essence of the three [other seals]: action seal, dharma seal, and pledge seal.[4]

There are many more such profound explanations. Generally, though, they do not take into account the full range of meanings for *mudrā*, which carry over to *mahāmudrā*.

In the context of the tantras, mahāmudrā is often part of a set of the four mudrās mentioned above: action seal (*karmamudrā*), dharma seal (*dharmamudrā*), pledge seal (*samayamudrā*), and great seal (*mahāmudrā*). A certain succession developed to these four in terms of progressive

realization, and they are related to the four empowerments in a highest yoga tantra initiation. Some recent scholarship on ancient Dunhuang manuscripts suggests that it wasn't always this order, that samayamudrā and mahāmudrā were reversed, with mahāmudrā referring only to the complete form of the deity.[5] Be that as it may, there is a long tradition of the progressive understanding in both Indian and Tibetan literature that emphasizes mahāmudrā as the ultimate realization of mind's nature, which is arrived at after experiencing the other mudrā practices in the context of a tantric initiation. Mudrā can also refer to a spiritual partner or consort, either real or imagined, depending on the stage of the initiation, union with whom leads to various experiences of bliss. Mahāmudrā, then, is only realized in the fourth and last empowerment, when the mahāmudrā consort is a spontaneous reflection of one's own mind and the ultimate union of bliss and emptiness is realized.

The highest yoga tantras where these teachings were primarily expounded arrived from India into Tibet during the second wave of Buddhist transmission and quickly became established. At the same time, esoteric instructions based on the tantras passed in person from living Indian masters to Tibetans, either in India itself or in Tibet. This exchange was the breeding ground for all the "new" (*gsar ma*) schools of Buddhism in Tibet, after which everything from the earlier spread was labeled as "ancient" (*snying ma*).

The Kagyü Treatment of Mahāmudrā

The Kagyü school traces its Tibetan lineage to Marpa Chökyi Lodrö (ca. 1010–ca. 1090), who traveled to India and received

teachings from extraordinary adepts, most notably Nāropa and Maitrīpa. Nāropa had received tantric transmissions from Tilopa, which were later formalized in a set of practices familiar as the Six Dharmas of Nāropa. The teachings that Marpa received from Maitrīpa, who had received them from the master Śavaripa, were mainly non-tantric instructions based on a practice of letting the mind settle in its own state, or mental nonengagement (*yid la mi byed pa*), that was being disseminated by the Indian mahāsiddhas. Of special note in this tradition was Saraha, whose teachings came to Tibet through the medium of dohās, a form of poetic composition in rhyming couplets, and other compositions.[6] Saraha is therefore considered the forefather of the Kagyü mahāmudrā practice that is mostly familiar now.

Marpa Lōtsawa brought back both sets of instructions and passed them to his disciples, notably the famous Milarepa, who in turn passed them on to Rechungpa and Gampopa. It was Gampopa Sönam Rinchen (1079–1153) who established monastic centers and incorporated these teachings with those of Atiśa's Kadampa lineage, which was mainly based on sutras and the gradual path, or *lam rim*. Gampopa gathered many disciples, some of them famous for being the founders of sub-orders, known as the four early and eight later Kagyü lineages. He also began to call the mahāsiddha teachings on mental nonengagement "mahāmudrā" and allowed his disciples to teach them around the vast country with only a consecration or authorization ritual of Vajravārāhī rather than a full four-fold tantric initiation, so that many disciples would have the opportunity to practice these essential Dharma teachings. Dakpo Tashi Namgyal (1512/13–1587), in his classic *Moonbeams of Mahāmudrā*, states:

> The teachers of this meditational lineage up to Milarepa meditated mainly on the key instructions of the Mantrayāna mysticism while at various times incorporating vital instructions on mahāmudrā from the discourses on the yogas of inner heat and lucid awareness. Yet the great master Gampopa, having been moved by immeasurable compassion, expounded mainly on the quintessential instructions on mahāmudrā. As a result, it became widely known as the single path for all predestined seekers.[7]

According to Jamgön Kongtrul, Gampopa continued to teach the tantric path of Nāropa's Six Dharmas as well as this "new" mahāmudrā that he says derived from the Kadampa lineage:

> [Gampopa] taught his regular disciples the Kadampa stages of the path and the meditative absorption from the tradition that is adorned with the name *mahāmudrā*. He taught the uncommon mahāmudrā of Mantra connected to Lama Mila's path of skillful methods to his extraordinary disciples.[8]

The essence of this mahāmudrā is very close indeed to that in the myriad sutras on the perfection of wisdom (*prajñāpāramitā*), so it eventually became known as "sutra mahāmudrā," as distinguished from the tantric mahāmudrā mentioned above. It became "adorned" (as in Kongtrul's careful word choice) by elements of a progressive path, with the

practices of calm abiding and higher insight as the foundation of the journey that leads through four stages of realization, known as the four yogas: one-pointedness, freedom from elaboration, single flavor, and nonmeditation. And thus it remains to the present day.

But back then, the brilliant if slightly puritanical scholar Sakya Paṇḍita Kunga Gyaltsen (1182–1251) was not at all happy with this development. The rebuttal that took aim directly at Gampopa and the Kagyü schools came in his famous text, *A Clear Differentiation of the Three Codes*, written around 1232.[9] This is a scathing assessment of the state of Buddhism, and particularly Vajrayāna in Tibet, barely disguised as a discussion of the three levels of vows. Sakya Paṇḍita's motivation was certainly to differentiate and separate those systems and to point out incidents and indiscretions of crossing over, inaccuracy, hybridity, and misapplication. But the polemic goes far beyond just that, and with his searing logic he calls into question many issues of lineage, appropriation, false advertising, false gurus, false empowerments, and everything else false about, particularly, the Kagyü. The gist of it was simple, as reported by Jamgön Kongtrul:

> Mahāmudrā is not designated in the tradition of the perfections. The pristine awareness of mahāmudrā only arises from empowerment.[10]

The response to this attack was...silence...for a few centuries, while it soaked in.[11] But by the fifteenth century the Kagyü defense was in full swing, responding to Sakya Paṇḍita's accusations and those of his later followers, such as Gorampa Sönam Sengé (1429–63).[12] The debate raged on, and seems to

show up in almost all the Kagyü commentaries of the time. There are very good and interesting points to be made, and it is both rewarding and fun to investigate these issues.

Having done that, to save you time, my conclusion is that Gampopa prevails in the end.[13] Why? Simply by virtue of the renown and popularity of "his" mahāmudrā, the so-called sutra and essence mahāmudrā that eclipsed all other versions in the popular mind and is now simply *the* mahāmudrā. And it is arguably the most useful. Not only that, it is clear that its authentic source is the tradition of Indian mahāsiddhas that is replete with such teachings, which both Tibetan scholars and academics have repeatedly demonstrated. Klaus-Dieter Mathes concludes:

> It should be noted that sūtra-based mahāmudrā teachings have Indian roots which can be clearly identified. To sum up, the blending of the Sūtras with the Tantras is something that definitely started in India and not in Tibet.[14]

And as the great Padma Karpo (1527–92) said, "Worrying about the reasons for [the Kagyüs] having it or not is like [worrying about] whether a rabbit's horns are sharp or dull." He confessed to being worn out by the whole thing.[15]

This mahāmudrā that reveals the true nature of one's own mind and thence that of all phenomena has been preeminent in all Kagyü lineages since then, along with the yogic teachings from Nāropa. One of the great disciples of Gampopa and Rechungpa was Düsum Khyenpa (1110–93). He became retroactively the first in a series of recognized reincarnations, the Karmapas, which is thought of as the earliest case of the now

ubiquitous tulku system of incarnate lamas. Düsum Khyenpa also marks the beginning of the Karma Kagyü suborder, also known as Kamtsang Kagyü. The second Karmapa, Karma Pakshi (1204–83), inherited the monasteries and authority of his predecessor.[16] The third Karmapa was Rangjung Dorjé (1284–1339), the author of the *Aspiration Prayer of Definitive Mahāmudrā.*

Karmapa Rangjung Dorjé

With all the schools and subschools, it might seem to be very systematic with everyone keeping in their own lane. In fact these early masters received and practiced instructions from many sources. Karmapa Rangjung Dorjé exemplifies this well. He composed widely on a variety of topics and is considered a preeminent figure not only in the Kagyü lineages but also those of Severance, or Chö (*gcod*), and Nyingma. He composed treatises that became the foundation for studies by generations of meditators and scholars in the Karma Kagyü tradition and beyond, ranging from the massive commentary on the highest yoga tantras, *The Profound Inner Principles* (*Zab mo nang don*), to condensed profound supplications such as the *Aspiration Prayer of Mahāmudrā.* Though this last stands on its own as a deep contemplative practice, it took a later Kagyü tulku, the great Situ Pema Nyinjé Chökyi Jungné, to unlock all that it contains in his commentary, *The Oral Transmission of the Supreme Siddhas.* This commentary is not only instructive, but the reverence that the author demonstrates for his ancestral Karmapa is abundantly evident and heartwarming. Mendong Tsampa Rinpoché likewise displays the same devotional attitude, one that has not diminished at all

with the years but seems to grow with each successive generation. Further commentary on these commentaries would be wholly redundant, but it is hoped the respect and devotion will continue to manifest in you, the readers.

Mendong Tsampa Rinpoché

Mendong Tsampa is an interesting character and almost our contemporary. I'm sure that many of the beloved Kagyü masters that my generation has been fortunate to meet must have met him or his students. One of those was the late Bokar Rinpoché, Karma Ngedön Chökyi Lodrö (1940–2004), the successor too briefly of Khyabjé Kalu Rinpoché in the Shangpa lineage. The Mendong and Bokar monasteries are close by each other in Tshochen (Coqen) county, Ngari prefecture, in western Tibet. It was Bokar Rinpoché who organized the printing of the three-volume collection of Mendong Tsampa's works. The following is a loose translation of the brief life story that Bokar Rinpoché included at the end of the third volume.

Lamp for the Minds of the Faithful: A Rough Sketch of the Activities of the Glorious Guru[17]
by Bokar Tulku Rinpoché

Your smiling face of all victors' compassion, like camphor pollen,
emanates in a single drop the signs and marks of the awakened,
ensuring the benefit and well-being of all great secret tantras:
I bow to the guru, skilled in inviting the four kāya guests.

Tsampa Rinpoché of Mendong Monastery in Tö (Gtod) was named Karma Ngedön Tengyé Mawai Sengé Palzangpo. In the upper snow ranges near Mount Tisé (Kailash), which was prophesied by the Victor as the celestial palace of Cakrasaṃvara in the mandala of the ḍākinīs of the three sacred sites, there is one of the nine tribes called Drongmé ('Brong smad). In the northeast of Drong, in the confluence of the vast valley, in a town called Makyayu (Ma skya yu) in the precious landscape, he was born in the year 1867 of the Western calendar; the earth female rabbit year of the fifteenth cycle. His stepfather was Trapun and his mother Josang Chödrön. After he was conceived, his mother dreamed of light radiating from her navel and filling all the land with light. Her body felt light and healthy, and many good omens occurred. After only seven months he was born amidst rainbows and brilliant lights appearing in the clear sky. He was given the name Jamyang Palden. While still young, he trained in letters and learned how to read and write. As he grew up, he naturally had a great affinity for the Dharma and had no desire to pursue this world. However, his parents, in accord with the general customs, invited a girl called Akar to be his bride. At twenty-five he had become very knowledgeable, so at the villagers' request he built a dwelling in the town. Like the father of a hundred children, he was always fair to everyone and became worthy of everyone's respect.

On one occasion, while traveling to the south, his horse was stolen and he decided to pursue the matter. The local minster held a trial, but the magistrate was biased in favor of the thief, so Rinpoché became very sad. He took the case to the central government in Lhasa to file a lawsuit. As a form of collateral, he offered horses and mules. The court came to a verdict about

the thief and they called for the local magistrate. Rinpoché's representative waited for the result in Lhasa. But that biased judge who had made his decision even before the trial was too ashamed to show up in court. So Rinpoché forfeited his horses and mules and went to Tsurphu Monastery [the main seat of the Karmapas].

At Tsurphu he met the fifteenth Gyalwang Karmapa, Khakhyab Dorjé (1870/71–1921/22), and gradually took the levels of monastic ordination. He studied sutras, tantras, and classical texts with many experts. He met the refuge lord Chöwang Tulku Rinpoché and received all the empowerments and instructions on the profound meaning of the great Secret Mantra Vehicle, like pouring all the contents from one pot into another. He became a master of all areas of knowledge. Through complete mastery of the paths of methods and liberation, he could control his own wind-mind. He became totally free of stains of the eight worldly concerns, or any kind of pretense. He kept silent for many years and sealed off his retreat place, passing the time in that way. He blazed in glory through his powers of knowledge and love. By speaking spontaneously he became a great orator.

He thought he should do something for the people, so he came back to the upper valley. By then he had become sick with gout, so he had to travel by yak wherever he was invited. After returning home, he spent time only in recitation retreat in a one-person tent. Life and practice had became identical. Between sessions, to fulfill students' wishes, he gave empowerments, guidance, and wrote commentaries on the treatises and oral instructions, creating a vast and profound body of work. He performed a special consecration in the beautiful

Vajra Court of the Bodhi Medicine Tree, the gathering place of the sangha.

The gout caused his legs to swell, but he would not treat it, so the swelling burst open to the point where the bones were visible. The area became infected and odorous, oozing dark pus. Rather than cleaning it, he took an oath of generosity to let bugs and maggots consume the rotting flesh. His lower body became all bony. To demonstrate impermanence, Mendong Tsampa Rinpoché passed away in the iron bird year (1921) at the age of eighty-two. The Karmapa gave the order not to cremate his body, but rather to enshrine it in a stupa with the face showing, as a seed of fortune for future disciples. Known as a special sublime support, it became famous as an object of liberation upon seeing.

He had many students, including his younger brother Khenchen Lungrik Gyaltsen, who became a great master. When he passed away, he was cremated and his ashes were divided between Mendong and Bokar Monasteries. The two younger sisters, the elder Kunzang Drolma and the younger Karma Chönyi, were also great practitioners. The latter passed away at ninety-four in a water horse year (1942) with her body shrunken to one cubit in length. Other students were Ane Chödzé Rinpoché, Drupön Sherab Thogmé, Drupön Karma Tsewang, Lhajé Yeshé Gyaltsen, Drupön Adamchö Rinpoché, Karma Döndam Gyurmé, and the amazing Lama Rapga Rinpoché.

This story was gathered from the oral accounts of scholars and ordinary old people who knew him. As firsthand accounts, nothing was made up or omitted. However, his commentaries and oral instructions were never before gathered in one

place and had remained scattered. Apart from that, if other scholars know more information on his amazing activities, including other information on dates, then they can add to this short account, which was written for the printing of his *Collected Works*.

Aspiration Prayer of Definitive Mahāmudrā

by Karmapa Rangjung Dorjé

Namo guru

1. Gurus and yidams, deities of the mandala,
victors of the ten directions and three times, and heirs,
consider me with love and bless me so my aspirations
will be accomplished just as intended.

2. A stream of virtues not muddied by the three spheres
descends the snow mountain of totally pure thoughts and
deeds,
mine and those of infinite sentient beings;
may it flow into the ocean of the victors' four kāyas.

3. Until that comes to pass, however long it takes,
throughout life after life in the future,
with even the sounds "sin" and "suffering" unknown;
may I enjoy the glorious sea of happiness and virtue.

4. Free and endowed; having faith, vigor, and wisdom,
attending a good spiritual master, receiving the nectar of teachings,
and properly practicing them without obstacles;
may I engage in the holy Dharma in all future lifetimes.

5. Studying scripture and logic liberates from obscurations of unknowing.
Contemplating esoteric instruction vanquishes doubt's darkness.
Light from meditation illuminates the abiding nature as it is.
May the brilliance of these three wisdoms increase.

6. "Ground" means the two truths free of extreme eternalism or nihilism.
"Supreme path" is two accumulations free of extreme imposition or denial.
This leads to the result: the two benefits free of extreme existence or peace.
May I meet the Dharma without deviation or error.

7. The ground of refining is mind itself, the unity of clarity-emptiness.
The refiner is the great vajra yoga of mahāmudrā.
It refines the object, the stains of incidental delusion.
May I actualize the refined result, stainless dharmakāya.

8. Deep confidence in the view is to sever impositions on the ground.
The vital point of meditation is to hold that without distraction.

Best conduct is to exercise skill in all meanings of
meditation.
May I have deep confidence in view, meditation, and
conduct.

9. All phenomena are projections of the mind.
As for mind, there is no mind—it is empty of an essence.
But, while empty, it appears freely as anything at all.
Examining this thoroughly, may I sever its base and roots.

10. Mind's displays that never existed are mistaken for
objects.
Innate awareness is ignorantly mistaken for a self.
We wander in the expanse of existence by such dualism.
May I get to the bottom of delusional mistakes.

11. It does not exist; even the victors don't see it.
It doesn't not exist; it's the basis of all samsara and nirvana.
No contradiction; it's the middle way of unity.
May I realize mind's true nature without extremes.

12. To say "this is" doesn't indicate anything.
To say "this is not" doesn't refute anything.
Unformed true nature defies the intellect.
May I gain certainty in the range of genuine reality.

13. Not to realize this is to flounder in samsara's ocean.
To realize it is nothing other than buddhahood.
Being all, "this is it" and "this is not it" mean nothing at all.
May I awaken to the true nature hidden in the all-ground.

14. As appearance is mind, so too emptiness is mind.
As realization is mind, delusion is also one's mind.
As birth is mind, so is cessation the mind.
May I sever all the impositions of mind.

15. Unspoiled by meditation with mind-made effort,
unmoved by the winds of everyday affairs,
knowing how to fall naturally in the uncontrived innate state;
may I skillfully maintain the practice of mind's meaning.

16. The waves of subtle and coarse thoughts subside in themselves.
The river of unmoved mind abides within itself.
Free of the murky stains of dullness and darkness,
may the unmoving ocean of calm abiding be steady.

17. When you look again and again for imperceptible mind,
you see distinctly the meaning of not seeing, just as it is.
Severing doubts about the meaning of being and nonbeing,
may I know my own unmistakable nature.

18. When you look at objects, there are no objects, you see mind.
Looking at mind, there is no mind; empty of essence.
Looking at both frees dualistic fixation in its own place.
May I realize lucid clarity, the abiding nature of mind.

19. Free of mental engagement; this is mahāmudrā.
Free of extremes; this is mahāmadhyamaka.
All-inclusive, it is also called mahāsandhi.
May I gain confidence that knowing one is realizing all.

20. The great bliss free of attachment is continuous.
Lucid clarity without fixation on attributes is free of obscuring veils.
Nonthought beyond intellect is spontaneously present.
May these experiences occur continuously without effort.

21. Attachment fixated on good experience subsides on its own.
Delusion of bad thought is naturally pure in basic space.
Ordinary mind is free of acceptance and rejection, loss and gain.
May I realize the truth of unembellished true reality.

22. Though the nature of migrators is ever buddha,
they fail to realize it and wander endlessly in samsara.
May unbearable compassion be born in my being
for endlessly suffering sentient beings.

23. Unimpeded energy of unbearable compassion is love,
the meaning of its empty essence exposed.
This supreme path of unity that never deviates;
may I meditate on this day and night without interruption.

24. With the eyes and clairvoyances produced by potent meditation,
sentient beings are matured and buddha fields refined.
Aspirations for accomplishing buddha qualities are fulfilled.
May I become buddha, the ultimate fulfillment, maturation, and refinement.

25. By the compassion of the ten-direction victors and their heirs,
and the power of whatever pure virtue there is,
may my pure aspirations and those of all beings
all be fulfilled just as intended.

The Aspiration Prayer of Definitive Mahāmudrā *is by Lord Rangjung Dorjé*

Ornament of Dakpo Kagyü Thought

Short Commentary on the
Mahāmudrā Aspiration Prayer

by Mendong Tsampa Rinpoché,
Karma Ngedön Tengyé

།ཨ། །ཕྱག་ཆེན་སྨོན་ལམ་གྱི་འགྲེལ་ཚུང་དུ་གས་བརྒྱད་དགོངས་རྒྱན།
ན་མོ་གུ་ཏ་མ་ཀ་ཧ་ཐ་ཏ་ཡེ། དངོས་ཀུན་ཁྱབ་བདག་དཔལ་ལྡན་རྡོ་རྗེ་
འཛིན། །དབྱིར་མེད་གོལ་བ་བཞི་ལྡན་སྒོམ་པོ་པ། །གང་དེའི་གསང་
གསུམ་དབང་འབྱོར་ཀློ་ཀ། །ཡབ་སྲས་བརྒྱད་པར་བཅས་ལ་གུས་
ཕྱག་འཚལ། །དུགས་བརྒྱད་གྱི་ཐོབ་རྒྱ་མཚོ་གཤེགས་པའི་ཕྱལ།
།ཟབ་ལམ་ཀུན་མཛུན་ཀུན་ལས་ཁྱད་འཕགས་པ། །ཁྱེན་ཆེན་རྡོད་
ལྡན་མོས་གུས་ཕྱག་ཆེན་གྱི། །སྨོན་ལམ་ཚིག་དོན་མདོ་ཙམ་རང་
ཉིད་ཀྱི། །དད་པའི་གསོས་སུ་དབྱེ་ལ་ཁྱིན་ཀྱིས་རྟོགས། །དེའང་རྒྱལ་
བའི་བསྟན་པའི་སྙིང་པོ་གང་ས་ཅན་གྱི་ལྷོངས་འདིར་སྐྱབ་བརྒྱད་
ཤིང་ཏུ་ཆེན་པོ་བརྒྱད་ཀྱི་མཚོག་རབ་མཁན་མེད་དུགས་པོ་བཀའ་
བརྒྱད་ཅེས་ཡོངས་སུ་གྲགས་པ་འདི་ཉིད་ལ་ཟབ་རྒྱས་ཀྱི་ཆོས་ཚུལ་
རྒྱ་མཚོ་མཐའ་ཡས་པ་ཞིག་མངའ་བ་ལས། ཕྱུགས་དམ་གྱི་གཙོ་པོ་
ཐབས་ལམ་ནུ་རོ་ཆོས་རྡུག་དང། གོལ་ལམ་ཕྱག་རྒྱ་ཆེན་པོ་གཉིས་ལ་
མཛད་པ་ལས། ཕྱི་མ་ཉིད་ཀྱི་དོན་ཆམས་ཐམས་ཅད་མཁྱེན་པ་རང་
བྱང་ཞབས་ཀྱིས་སྨོན་ལམ་གྱི་ཚུལ་དུ་རྗེས་འཇུག་ཆམས་ལ་ཕྱུགས་
བཅོ་བས་གདམས་པར་མཛད་པ་འདིའི་ཚོག་དོན་བོལ་ཕྱི་ཙམ་གོ
ན་ཅང། མ་རྟོགས་རྟོགས་པར་བྱེད་ཅིང། རྟོགས་པ་བོགས་དབྱུང་བའི
གདམས་ངག་གི་གནད་བླ་མེད་དུ་གསུངས་པས། དེ་ལ་ས་བཅད
གསུམ། སྨྱོར་བ། དངོས་གཞི། རྗེས་སོ། །

Namo guru mahāmudrāya

Glorious Vajradhara, all-pervading sovereign,
inseparable from Gampopa, having four liberations,[18]
and Karmapa, master of his three secrets;
I bow in devotion to father and son with their lineage.

The road traveled by an ocean of Dakpo Kagyü adepts,
the profound path that agrees with all yet is superior to all,
possessing the blessing of warmth, is devotional mahāmudrā.
I will briefly summarize the meaning of its aspiration
so that I may receive blessings to refresh my faith.

The heart of the Victor's doctrine manifests here in the Land of Snows as the eight great chariots of the practice lineages. Foremost among them is renowned as the incomparable Dakpo Kagyü. In this one finds an infinite ocean of profound and vast Dharma systems. Among them, the two principal spiritual practices that were created are the methods path of the Six Dharmas of Nāropa and the liberation path of Mahāmudrā. Omniscient Rangjung has revealed the meaning of the latter in the style of an aspiration prayer out of kindness for his followers. Although we have a vague sense of its meaning, this unsurpassed instruction in the vital points was taught to produce new realization and enhance what has been realized. There are three parts: preparation, main part, and conclusion.

དང་པོ་རྟོག་བཤད།

ན་མོ་ཀུ་བཏ། བླ་མ་ཆོས་དང་ཡི་དམ་དཀྱིལ་འཁོར་ལྷ། ཁྱོགས་བཅུ་
དུས་གསུམ་རྒྱལ་བ་སྲས་དང་བཅས། །བདག་ལ་བཟོད་དགོངས་
བདག་གི་སྨོན་ལམ་ཆོས། །ཇི་བཞིན་འགྲུབ་པའི་མཐུན་འགྱུར་བྱིན་
བརླབས་མཛོད།

།ཅེས་གསུངས་ཏེ། སྨོན་ལམ་གེགས་མེད་དུ་འགྲུབ་པའི་ཚེད་དུ་ཡུལ་
ཁྱད་པར་འཕགས་པ་ཆོས་དཔང་པོར་གསོལ་ཞིང་དེའི་རྒྱང་དུ་
འདུན་པ་ཙེ་གཅིག་པས་སྨོན་ལམ་གདབ་དགོས་པར་འདོད་མས་པ་སྟེ།
མདོ་ལས། ཚོས་ཆོས་ཐམས་ཅད་ཀྱིན་བཞིན་དུ། །འདུན་པའི་ཙེ་ལ
རབ་ཏུ་གནས། །གང་གིས་སྨོན་ལམ་ཅི་བཏབ་པ། །འཕྲས་བུ་དེ་འདྲ
བོ་ནར་སྨིན། །ཞེས་གསུངས་པས་སོ། །

གཉིས་པ་སྨོན་ལམ་དངོས་ལ། སྨྱ་དང། ཏེ་ཐུག་གཉིས་ལས། དང་པོ
ས্ম্ব্ব্ব

I. Preparation

Namo guru

1. *Gurus and yidams, deities of the mandala,*
victors of the ten directions and three times, and heirs,
consider me with love and bless me so my aspirations
will be accomplished just as intended.

In order to **accomplish** your **aspirations** without obstruction, this prayer encourages you to solicit an especially elevated object as a witness and in their presence make your aspiration with undivided intent. It states in a sutra:

> As all phenomena are conditioned,
> they fully rest on the basis of intent.
> Whatever aspiration anyone makes,
> the fruit can only ripen accordingly.[19]

II. Main part

In the main aspiration, there are both general and particular explanations.

A. The general dedication of virtue to perfect awakening

2. *A stream of virtues not muddied by the three spheres,*
descends the snow mountain of totally pure thoughts and deeds,
mine and those of infinite sentient beings;
may it flow into the ocean of the victors' four kāyas.

ཅེས་གསུངས་ཏེ། བདག་དང་མཐའ་ཡས་པའི་སེམས་ཅན་ཐམས་
ཅད་ཀྱི་དུག་གསུམ་གྱི་སེམས་དང་མ་འདྲེས་པར་བྱམས་བཟོ་དང་
མོས་སོགས་ཀྱིས་ཀུན་ནས་བསླང་བས་བསམ་པ་ཆེམ་པར་དག
པ་དང། ཕྱི་ནང་མ་འདྲེས་པ་སོགས་ཀྱི་སྟོང་བ་ཆེམ་དག་གིས
བསྒྲབས་པའི་ཆེམ་པར་དགར་བའི་ལས་དྲི་མེད་གང་རས་ཝ་ལྟ་བུ
ལས་སྐྱེས་པའི། ཡུལ་དང་དངོས་པོ་བྱེད་པ་སྟེ་འཁོར་གསུམ་ཀྱི
དམིགས་པའི་རྣལ་ཀྱིས་ཆོ་ག་མེད་པའི་དགེ་ཚོགས་ཀྱི་ཚུ་རྒྱུན
ཆམས་གང་དུ་གཞོལ་ཞིང་འབབ་པའི་ཡུལ་ཆོས་སྐུ་ལོངས་སྐུ་སྤྲུལ
སྐུ་བདེ་བ་ཆེན་པོ་ངོ་བོ་ཉིད་སྐུ་སྟེ། རྒྱལ་བ་ཆམས་ཀྱི་སྐུ་བཞིའི་ངོ
བོ་ནི་ཟབ་ཅིང་རྒྱ་ཆེ་བས་རྒྱ་མཚོ་ལྟ་བུ་ཏེར་འདུག་པར་ཀྱུར་ཅིག
ཅེས་བསྟོ་དགོས་པར་འདོམ་པའི་ཕྱིར་སྟོན་པར་མཛད་པ་སྟེ་ཕྱི་མ
ཆམས་ལའང་ཤེས་པར་བྱའོ། །འཁོར་གསུམ་དམིགས་བཟལ་ཀྱི་ཤེས
རབ་དངོས་ནི་འཕགས་པའི་སྟོང་ཡུལ་ཡིན་ཀྱང་ལུང་དང་བློ་མའི
གདམས་ངག་གིས་ཇེས་མཐུན་ཏོགས་པ་ནི་སོ་སྐྱེ་ལའང་ཡོད་པར
གསུངས།

གཉིས་པ་བྱེ་བྲག་ཕྱི་སྟེ་སྟོན་པ་ལ་ལྔ། ལམ་ཀྱི་རྟེན་ཕུན་ཚོགས་ལ
སྟོན་པ། ལམ་རྟོགས་བྱེད་ཀྱི་ཤེས་རབ་ལ་སྟོན་པ། འགྲུལ་མེད་ཀྱི
ལམ་ལ་སྟོན་པ། ལམ་དེའི་ཉམས་ལེན་མ་འགྲུལ་བ་ལ་སྟོན་པ། ལམ
མཐར་ཕྱིན་པའི་འབྲས་བུ་ལ་སྟོན་པའོ། །དང་པོ་ལ་ཕུན་མོང་དང
ཕུན་མིན་གཉིས་ལས། དང་པོ་ ཕུན་མོང་ལམ་ཀྱི་རྟེན་ཕུན་ཚོགས་ལ
སྟོན་པ་དེ།

My totally pure thoughts and those of infinite sentient beings that are motivated by love, affection, faith, devotion, and so on, that are not mixed with a **mind** afflicted by three poisons, and the accomplishment of **totally pure deeds** not mixed with negativity and such, are totally white, immaculate karma like **the snow mountain**. Regarding place and things, **a stream** is the collected **virtues** that are **not muddied by** the sediment of reference to **the three spheres** of recipient, thing, and act. The place into which they fall is the dharmakāya, saṃbhogakāya, nirmāṇakāya, and mahāsukha svabhāvakāya. Since the essence of those **four kāyas** of all the **victors** is profound and vast, it is like **the ocean**. "**May it flow into** there" is the aspiration in order to encourage the necessary dedication. Know that this applies to all the future aspirations. Although the actual wisdom free of reference to the three spheres is the realm of activity of the noble ones, it is taught that a comparable realization based on the scriptures and guru's instructions are achieved by ordinary individuals.

B. The distinguishing particular explanations

These are divided into five: (1) aspiration for excellent support for the path, (2) aspiration for the wisdom that produces realization on the path, (3) aspiration for an undeluded true path, (4) aspiration for unmistaken practice on that path, and (5) aspiration for the ultimate result of the path.

(1) Aspiration for excellent support for the path

This has two parts: common and uncommon.

རྗེ་གྲྭ་དེ་མ་ཐོབ་པ་དེ་གྲྭ་དུ། །རྒྱུ་དང་རྒྱུ་བ་ཚོ་རབས་ཀུན་ཏུ་
ཡང། །ལྷག་དང་ལྷག་བསྟལ་སྒྲ་ཡང་མི་གྲགས་ཅིང། །བདེ་དགེ་རྒྱ
མཚོའི་དཔལ་ལ་སྒྲོད་པར་མཛོད

།ཅེས་གསུངས་ཏེ། འདི་ནས་བཟུང་སྟེ་རྗེ་ཅམ་གྲྭ་པར་རྒྱུ་ཞིང་རྒྱལ
བ་སྐུ་བཞིའི་གོ་འཕང་དམ་པ་དེ་མ་ཐོབ་པ་དེ་གྲྭ་ཀྱི་བར་དུ་རྒྱུ
དང་རྒྱུ་བའི་ཚོ་རབས་ཀུན་ཏུ་ཡང་རྒྱུ་ལྷག་པ་དང་འབྲས་བུ་ལྷག
བསྟལ་ཀྱི་སྒྲ་ཅམ་ཡང་མི་གྲགས་ཅིང་བདེ་ཞིང་རྒྱུ་ལྡན་པ་དང་དེའི་རྒྱ
དགེ་བ་རྒྱ་མཚོ་ལྟ་བུའི་དཔལ་འབྱོར་ལ་ལོངས་སྤྱོད་པ་ཁོ་ན་ཤོག
ཅེག་ཅེས་པའོ། །

གཉིས་པ་ ཕྱུན་མིན་ལམ་གྱི་རྟེན་ཕུན་ཚོགས་ལ་སྨོན་པ། ནི

དལ་འབྱོར་མཚོག་ཐོབ་དང་བཙོན་ཤེས་རབ་ལྟན། །བཤེས་གཉེན
བཟང་བསྟེན་གདམས་པའི་བཅུད་ཐོབ་ནས། །ཚུལ་བཞིན་བསྒྲུབ་ལ
བར་ཆད་མ་མཆིས་པར། །ཚོ་རབས་ཀུན་ཏུ་དམ་ཚོས་སྒྲོད་པར་ཤོག

།ཅེས་གསུངས་ཏེ། དེར་མ་ཟད་ཁྱད་པར་དུ་ཡང་བྱང་ཆུབ་བསྒྲུབ
བྱང་གི་རྟེན་དལ་བཅུད་འབྱོར་བཅུ་ཚང་བའི་ཁམས་དྲུག་ལྟན་གྱི
མིའི་ལུས་མཚོག་ཁོ་ན་ཐོབ་ཅིང། རྟེན་འབྲེང་གི་ཆོས་ལས་འབྲས་ལ
ཡིད་ཆེས་པའི་དད་པ། ས་ངས་རྒྱས་ཀྱི་བྱང་ཆུབ་ལ་འདོད་པའི་དད
པ། བླ་མ་དགོན་མཚོག་ལ་དང་བའི་དད་པ་དང། དགེ་བ་ལ་ཆེས
སྒོ་བའི་རྩ་གསུམ་སྒྲོར་དང། ཀུས་སྒྲོར་ཀྱི་བཙོན་འགྲུས་དང། འཇིག་རྟེན
དང་འཇིག་རྟེན་ལས་འདས་པའི་ཤེས་བྱའི་ཆོས་ཐམས་ཅད་རབ

a. Common aspiration

3. *Until that comes to pass, however long it takes,*
throughout life after life in the future,
with even the sounds "sin" and "suffering" unknown;
may I enjoy the glorious sea of happiness and virtue.

From now on **until however long it takes** to attain that sublime state of the victors' four kāyas, **throughout life after life in the the future**, we pray that **even the sounds** of the causal **sins** and the resultant **sufferings** be **unknown**, while **enjoying** only prosperity and **glorious happiness** and joy and their cause, which is like a **sea of virtue**.

b. Uncommon aspiration

4. *Free and endowed; having faith, vigor, and wisdom,*
attending a good spiritual master, receiving the nectar of teachings,
and properly practicing them without obstacles;
may I engage in the holy Dharma in all future lifetimes.

Not only that, you especially aspire to obtain only the support conducive to accomplishing awakening, which is the excellent human body with six constituents, and including all eight **freedoms and** ten **endowments**. You aspire to have [three kinds of faith:] the **faith** of belief in the functioning of cause and effect in interdependently arising phenomena, the faith of yearning for a buddha's awakening, and the faith of inspiration in the guru and Three Jewels. You aspire to have the **vigor** of constant application and devoted application to

ཏུ་འཕྲིད་ནས་ཀྱི་ཤེས་རབ་ཆུམས་དང་ལྡན་པ་དང། བློ་མེད་རྫོགས་
བྱང་དུ་འཕྲིད་པའི་ལམ་མཁན་བློ་མ་དམ་པ་དགེ་བའི་བཤེས་གཉེན་
མཚན་ཉིད་དང་ལྡན་པའི་བཟང་པོ་དང་ཕྱད་ནས་དེ་ཉིད་མཉེས་
པའི་ཞབས་ཏོག་དགུ་ཕྲུগས་སོགས་མདོར་ན་བློ་མ་ལྟ་བཅུ་པ་ལས་
གསུངས་པ་ལྟར་ཚུལ་བཞིན་ཏུ་བསྟེན་པས། དེ་ཉིད་ལས་གདུལ་
བྱའི་ཁམས་དབང་དང་འཚམས་པའི་གདམ་ངག་ཐར་ལམ་གྱི་སྒོག
འཛིན་པའི་བཅུད་ལྡན་པ་ཐོབ་ནས་ཐོབ་ལོ་ཅམ་དུ་མི་འཇོག་པར
ཇི་སྐད་གདམས་པའི་ཚུལ་དེ་ཁོ་ན་བཞིན་དུ་བསྒྲུབ་ཅིང་ཉམས
སུ་ལེན་པ་དང། དེ་ལ་ཕྱི་འབྱུང་བ་བཞི་དང་མི་མ་ཡིན་སོགས་ཀྱི
བར་ཆད་དང། ནང་ནད་དང་ཉོན་མོངས་ཆུམ་པར་རྟོག་པ་སོགས
མདོར་ན་བྱང་ཆུབ་ཀྱི་ལམ་ལ་བར་ཆད་མཐའ་དག་མ་མཆིས་པར
ཚོ་རབས་ཀྱི་ཕྲིང་བ་ཀུན་ཏུ་དམ་ཆོས་ཆུལ་མ་ལ་སྟོང་པའི་སྐལ་བ
ཅན་ཁོ་ནར་འགྱུར་བར་ཤོག་ཅིག་ཅེས་པའོ།།

གཉིས་པ་ལམ་རྟོགས་བྱེད་ཀྱི་ཤེས་རབ་ལ་སྟོན་པ་ནི།

ལྷང་རིགས་ཐོས་པས་མི་ཤེས་སྒྲིབ་ལས་གྲོལ། །མན་ངག་བསམ་པས
ཐེ་ཚོམ་སྲུན་ནས་བཅོམ། །བསྒོམས་བྱང་འོད་ཀྱིས་གནས་ལྷགས་ཤེ
བཞིན་གསལ། །ཤེས་རབ་གསུམ་གྱི་སྣང་བ་རྒྱས་པར་ཤོག།

eagerly pursue virtue. You aspire to have **wisdom** that can fully distinguish all mundane and transcendent knowable phenomena. Endowed with all those, you aspire to meet the guide who leads you to unsurpassed complete awakening, a holy guru with all the characteristics of **a good spiritual master**, and then offer all kinds of pleasing service and so on. This is, briefly, to **attend** that master properly according to the instructions in *Fifty Verses of Guru Devotion*.[20] From that person, the disciple **receives the** vitalizing **nectar** of the path to freedom as a **teaching** that is compatible with your constitution and capabilities. Once you obtain it, do not become complacent in thinking "I've got it." **Put it into practice properly** and accomplish it only in the way in which it was taught, **without** any external **obstacles** from the four elements or nonhumans and so forth, and without inner **obstacles** such as sickness, afflictions, and discursive thoughts. In short, we aspire only to become a fortunate one who **engages** in the genuine **holy Dharma** throughout the succession of **all future lifetimes**, free of all obstacles to the path of awakening.

(2) Aspiration for the wisdom that produces realization on the path

5. *Studying scripture and logic liberates from obscurations of unknowing.*
Contemplating esoteric instruction vanquishes doubt's darkness.
Light from meditation illuminates the abiding nature as it is.
May the brilliance of these three wisdoms increase.

ཅེས་གསུངས་ཏེ། རྟོགས་པའི་སངས་རྒྱས་ཀྱི་ཞལ་ནས་གསུངས་པ་
རྣམས་སུ་གནང་བ་བྱིན་གྱིས་རླབས་པའི་བཀའ་གསུམ་མམ། བརྟོད་
བྱའི་དབང་དུ་ནི་སྟེ་སྟོང་གསུམ་སྟེ་བཀའ་དང། དེའི་དགོངས་འགྲེལ
གྱི་དང་བྱ་བྱག་སོགས་བསྟན་བཅོས་ཀྱི་ལུང་དང། ཚད་མའི་དམ
བཅའ་དང་གཏན་ཚིགས་དང་དཔེ་སོགས་ཀྱི་སྒོ་ནས་གཏན་ལ་ཕབ
པས་རྟོགས་བྱ་གང་ཡིན་ཀྱི་དོན་སྤྱིའི་ཚུལ་གྱིས་ཤེས་བྱེད་རིགས་པ
བཅས་བློ་མ་ལས་ཐོས་པར་བྱས་པས་ཐོས་བྱང་གི་ཤེས་རབ་སྐྱེས
ཏེ། དེའི་མི་མཐུན་ཕྱོགས་ལུང་རིགས་མི་ཤེས་པའི་སྒྲིབ་པ་ལས་གཞོལ
བ་དང། མདོ་རྒྱུད་དགོངས་འགྲེལ་དང་བཅས་པའི་དོན་དྲང་ངེས
དགོངས་ལྡེམ་དགོངས་དང་ཁྱད་པར་བློ་མེད་ཀྱི་རྒྱུད་མཐའ་དྲུག
ཚུལ་བཞིས་བཅིངས་པ་ཆུམས་མཚན་ལྡན་བློ་མས་ཚུལ་བཞིན་ཕྱིས
ཏེ་གདམས་པའི་མན་ངག་ཆུམས་རང་རྒྱུད་དང་སྒྲར་ཏེ་ཚུལ་བཞིན
བསམ་པས་བསམ་བྱང་གི་ཤེས་རབ་སྐྱེས་ཏེ་དེའི་ལྟོག་ཕྱོགས་ཟབ
མོའི་གནས་ལ་སེམས་ཅི་གཉིས་པའི་ཐེ་ཚོམ་གྱི་མུན་ནག་བཅོམ་པ
དང། མང་དུ་ཐོས་ཤིང་དོན་ཚུལ་བཞིན་བསམ་པས་ངེས་པ་ཉིད
པ་དེ་ཉིད་ལ་ཅི་གཅིག་ཏུ་མཉམ་པར་བཞག་ཅིང་གོམས་པར་བྱས
པས་སྒོམ་བྱང་གི་ཤེས་རབ་སྐྱེས་ཏེ་དེའི་འོད་ཀྱིས་གཟུགས་ནས་ཆུམ
མཁྱེན་བར་གྱི་ཚོས་ཐམས་ཅད་ཀྱི་རང་བཞིན་ནམ་གནས་ལུགས་དེ
ཉིད་ཇི་ལྟ་བ་བཞིན་དུ་གསལ་བ་དང། དེ་ལྟར་ཐོས་བསམ་སྒོམ་བྱང
གི་ཤེས་རབ་གསུམ་གྱི་རང་འོད་སྣང་བ་ཆེན་པོ་ཤིན་ཏུ་རྒྱས་པས་དེ
ཁོ་ན་ཉིད་ཀྱི་རང་བཞིན་མངོན་སུམ་དུ་མཐོང་བར་ཤོག་ཅེས་ཅེས
པའོ།

There are three kinds of Buddha Word: the words spoken directly by the perfect Buddha, those of which he approved, and those with his blessing. Or, in terms of subject matter, there are the three baskets (*Tripiṭaka*) of precepts, as well as the treatises that comment in general and in particular on their intent. This is **scripture. Logic** is to ascertain the truth by means of the logical theses of valid cognition, syllogisms, metaphors, and so on, that enable you to understand in a general fashion the meaning of whatever is to be realized. The wisdom that comes from **studying** with the guru arises and you are **liberated** from its opposite, the **obscuration** of **not knowing** scripture and logic.

An authentic guru distinguishes the meaning of sutras, tantras, and their commentaries as definitive, provisional, intentional, or having concealed intentions. Especially with regard to the highest yoga tantra, [the guru applies] the clinchers of the six limits and four modes.[21] The [disciple] applies those teachings of **esoteric instructions** to their own mindstream and properly **contemplates** them, giving rise to the wisdom that comes from contemplation, and **vanquishes** its opposite, the **darkness of** conflicted **doubt** concerning profound topics.

You will find certitude through much studying and proper contemplation of the meaning. The wisdom that comes **from meditation** will arise through resting in single-focused equipoise on just that and becoming accustomed to it. Its **light** will **illuminate** the intrinsic nature of all phenomena, from form up through omniscience, or **the abiding nature** of suchness **just as it is**. Thus, we aspire to see the intrinsic nature of suchness through the vast **increase** of great brilliance of the innate light of the **three wisdoms** that come from study, contemplation, and meditation.

།དེ་འང་གཞི་དུས་ཀྱི་ཕྱག་ཆེན། གཏུག་མའི་དེ་ཉིད། དང་པོའི་མཚོན་པོ། སེམས་ཀྱི་རྩོ་རྗེ། བདེ་གཤེགས་སྙིང་པོ་སོགས་རྣམ་གྲངས་དུ་མས་བསྟན་པ་དེ་ཉིད་ལའང་ལུས་དངོས་པོའི་གནས་ལུགས་དང་སེམས་དངོས་པོའི་གནས་ལུགས་གཉིས་ལས། ཐུ་མ་ནི་ཀུན་ཟོང་བྱང་སེམས་ལས་གྲུབ་པ་སྟང་བ་མཆོག་ཏུ་མི་འགྱུར་བའི་བདེ་བའི་རྒྱན་ཙ་ཏྲུང་ཕིག་ལེའི་དྭངས་མ་རྣལ་གྱི་ཚོས་ལས་འདས་པས་ཡེ་ཤེས་ཀྱི་ངོ་བོར་གྱུར་པ་གཏུག་མའི་ལུས་དང་རྒྱས་འགྱུར་གྱི་རིགས་ཞེས་ཚོས་རྗེ་ཀན্ས་པ་ཡབ་སྲས་བཞེད་ཅིང། ཕྱི་མ་ནི་རྒྱ་ཆད་ཟློག་ལྷུང་གི་ལྟོས་མཐའ་བྲལ་བའི་ཚོས་དབྱིངས་ཟབ་གསལ་གཉིས་མེད་གཏུག་མའི་སེམས་དང་རང་བཞིན་གནས་རིགས་ཞེས་པ་ཉིད་དེ་ལུས་སེམས་ཀྱི་གཞིའི་གནས་ལུགས་དེ་གཉིས་ཆུ་དང་འཁྱག་སྒྲམ་བཞིན་དབྱེར་མི་ཕྱེད་པས་གཞི་དུས་ཀྱི་སྣུ་གཉིས་ཟུང་འཇུག་ཅེས་བྱ་ཞིང། དེ་ཉིད་ཕྱིན་ཆད་བདང་སྒོམ་སྟོབས་ཀྱི་རང་རིག་མངོན་སུམ་ཁོ་ནས་གསལ་བར་ཕུས་ཀྱི་ཐབས་གཞན་ཀྱིས་མ་ཡིན་པར་གསུངས་སོ། །

གསུམ་པ་འབྲེལ་མེད་ཀྱི་ལམ་ཉིད་ལ་སྟོན་པ་ནི།

རྟག་ཆད་མཐའ་བྲལ་བདེན་གཉིས་གཞི་ཡི་དོན། །སྒྲོ་སྐུར་མཐའ་བྲལ་ཚོགས་གཉིས་ལམ་མཆོག་གིས། །སྲིད་ཞིའི་མཐའ་བྲལ་དོན་གཉིས་འབྲས་ཐོབ་པའི། །ཞོལ་འཛུག་མེད་པའི་ཚོས་དང་འཕྲད་པར་ཤོག

There are many synonyms that have been used, such as ground-state mahāmudrā, innate suchness, original lord, mind vajra, buddha nature, and so forth. Also there is the abiding nature of the body entity and the abiding nature of the mind entity. The former refers to the support of penultimate bliss that appears through relative bodhicitta—the refined essence of the channels, vital winds, and vital drops that transcend material phenomena and so are essentially timeless awareness. That is called the "innate body" (*gnyug ma'i lus*) and "developed affinity" (*rgyas 'gyur gyi rigs*), as explained by the lord Karmapa, father and sons. The latter is the realm of phenomena free of the limits of elaborations, partiality, and prejudice; the nondual profundity and clarity, also called "innate mind" and "the intrinsically abiding affinity." Those two abiding natures of the ground of body and mind are indivisible, like water and ice. So they are called "the unity of the two kāyas at the ground state." It is said that this itself can only be illuminated through reflexive awareness manifested by blessings and the power of meditation, and not by any other means.

(3) Aspiration for an undeluded path

6. *"Ground" means the two truths free of extreme eternalism or nihilism.*
"Supreme path" is two accumulations free of extreme imposition or denial.
This leads to the result: the two benefits free of extreme existence or peace.
May I meet the Dharma without deviation or error.

།ཅིས་གསུངས་ཏེ། དོན་དམ་བདེན་པ་བརྟན་གཡོ་འགོར་འདས་ཀྱི་
ཚོས་གང་སྟང་ཐམས་ཅད་སྟང་དུས་ཉིད་ནས་དེའི་ངོ་བོར་ཡོད་
མ་ཐྱོང་བ་མེ་ལོང་གི་གཟུགས་བརྙན་ལྟ་བུར་རྒྱ་བའི་མཐའ་དང་
བྲལ་ཞིང། ཀུན་ཇོག་བདེན་པ་ངོ་བོ་སྟོང་ཉིད་ལས་མ་གཡོས་བཞིན་
དུ་སྟང་བ་སྟ་ཚོགས་འགག་མེད་དུ་འཆར་བས་ཆད་པའི་མཐའ་
དང་བྲལ་བའི་བདེན་གཉིས་གཅོད་ནས་ཟུང་དུ་འཇུག་པའི་ཤེས་
བྱ་གཞིའི་གནས་ལུགས་ཀྱི་དོན་འཁྲུལ་མེད་དུ་རྟོགས་པ་དང། སྟང་
བའི་ཚོས་ཀོ་ནར་ཞེན་ནས་སྟོང་ཉིད་ལས་རྣེན་འབྱེལ་དུ་ཤར་ཚུལ
མ་ཤེས་པར་ཤེས་རབ་ཀྱི་ཚ་སྟོང་བ་མེད་པ་ལ་ཡོད་པར་སྟོ་བཏགས
པའི་མཐའ་དང། སྟོང་ཉིད་ཀོ་ནར་ཞེན་ནས་དཀོན་མཆོག་ལས
འབྱས་སོགས་རྣེན་འབྱུང་གི་ཚོས་སྟང་ངོ་ཙམ་དུ་དོན་བྱེད་ནུས་ཀྱི
གནད་མ་ཤེས་པར་ཐབས་ཀྱི་ཚ་སྟོང་བ་ཡོད་པ་ལ་མེད་པར་སྣུར
འདེབས་ཀྱི་མཐའ་སྟེ་མཐའ་དེ་གཉིས་དང་བྲལ་བས་ཐབས་བསོད
ནམས་ཀྱི་ཚོགས་དང་ཤེས་རབ་ཡེ་ཤེས་ཀྱི་ཚོགས་ཏེ་ཚོགས་གཉིས
ཕྱོགས་རིས་མེད་པར་ཟུང་འཇུག་ཏུ་བསྒྲུབ་པ་བླ་མེད་བྱང་ཆུབ
འཐོབ་པའི་ལམ་མཆོག་ཏུ་ཕྱིར་པ་དག་གིས། ཕྱིད་པའི་མཐར་མ
ལྟུང་བ་རང་དོན་ཕུན་ཚོགས་གཟུགས་ཀྱི་སྐུ་དང། ཞི་བའི་མཐར་མ
ལྟུང་བ་གཞན་དོན་ཕུན་ཚོགས་གཟུགས་ཀྱི་སྐུ་སྟེ་འབྱས་བུ་སྐུ་གཉིས
ཟུང་འཇུག་ཐོབ་པའི་གནད་གཞི་ལམ་འབྱས་གསུམ་ཀྱི་མཐའ་གཉིས
དང་བྲལ་ཏེ་གོལ་འཚུག་མེད་པའི་ཚོས་ཡང་དག་པ་དང་དེ་སྟོན
པའི་བླ་མ་དམ་པ་དང་འཕྲད་པར་ཤོག་ཅིག་ཅེས་པའོ།།

The ultimate truth is that one cannot experience the existence of an essence in any appearing phenomena of samsara and nirvana, animate or inanimate, from the very moment that they appear, as with the reflections in a mirror. This is **freedom from the extreme of eternalism**. The relative truth is that various appearances arise unhindered without actually shifting away from their empty essence. This is freedom from the **extreme of nihilism**. The knowledge that these two truths are united from the beginning is the undeluded realization of the **meaning of the ground**'s abiding nature.

Cleaving only to apparent phenomena while neglecting the wisdom aspect without understanding the way that interdependence arises from emptiness is the **extreme** of **superimposition** that imposes existence on nonexistence. Cleaving only to emptiness while neglecting the method aspect, and thinking that the Three Jewels and karmic cause and effect and such are merely the apparent phenomena of interdependence without understanding the vital point of their functionality, is the **extreme** of **denial** that denies the existence of what exists. **Free of** those **two extremes**, the practice of the **two accumulations**—the accumulation of merit and the accumulation of wisdom-awareness—as a unity without bias is the **supreme path** for attaining unsurpassed awakening.

Those who [follow that path] do not fall into the **extreme of** [conditioned] **existence** and attain the dharmakāya of abundant **benefit** for themselves, and do not fall into the **extreme of peace** and attain the rūpakāya of abundant benefit for others. The vital point is the attainment of **the result**: two kāyas united. Free of the dualistic extremes of all the three—ground, path, and result—we aspire to **meet** the genuine **Dharma without deviation or error** and the holy guru who teaches it.

བཞི་པ་ལམ་དེའི་ཁམས་སུ་ལེན་ཚུལ་མ་འགྲུལ་བར་སྨོན་པ་ལ་
གཉིས། གོ་དོན་དང། སྒོམ་དོན་ནོ། །དང་པོ་ཁོ་དོན་རེ།

སྒྲུབ་གཞི་ཞེམས་ཉིད་གསལ་སྟོང་ཟུང་འཇུག་ལ། །སྒྲོང་བྱེད་ཕྱག་ཆེན་རྟོ་རྗེའི་རྣལ་འབྱོར་ཆེས། །སྒྲུབ་བྱ་གློ་བུར་འགྲུལ་པའི་དྲི་མ་རྣམས། །སྒྲུབས་འབྲས་དྲི་བཟལ་ཆོས་སྐུ་མངོན་འགྱུར་ཨོཾ

།ཅེས་གསུངས་ཏེ། འཕོར་བར་འགྲུལ་བའི་དྲི་མ་སྒྲུབ་བའི་གཞི་ནི། སྟོང་དཔོན་ཀླུ་ཞབས་ཀྱིས། ས་བོན་ཀྱུར་པའི་ཁམས་དེ་ཉིད། ।ཆོས་རྣམས་ཀུན་གྱི་རྩེན་དུ་འདོད། ।རིམ་གྱིས་སྒྲུབས་པར་ཀྱུར་པ་ལས། ।ས་ངམས་རྒྱས་གོ་འཕང་འཐོབ་པར་ཀྱུར། ।ཞེས་སོགས་ལུང་མཐའ་ཡས་པའི་ཁམས་ས་མ་གཤེགས་སྙིང་ངམ་ས་མེམས་ཉིད་ཀྱི་རྩོ་རྗེ་ཞེས་པ་རང་བཞིན་འགག་མེད་དུ་གསལ་ཡང་ངོ་བོ་གཞི་མེད་ཙུ་བྱལ་དུ་སྟོང་པའི་གསལ་སྟོང་ཟུང་འཇུག་གི་མཚན་ཉིད་ཅན་དེ་ཡིན་ལ། དེའི་སྟེང་གི་དྲི་མ་སྒྲོང་བྱེད་ཀྱི་ཐབས་ནི་འདིར་ཤིང་རྟ་ཆེན་པོ་མཁན་མེད་དུ་གས་པོ་བཀའ་བརྒྱད་ཀྱི་གདམས་སྲོལ་ཕྱག་ཆེན་རྩོ་རྗེའི་རྣལ་འབྱོར་ཆེན་པོས་བདེ་བློ་ཏུ་སྒྲོང་སྟེ། སྒྲུབ་བར་བྱ་རྒྱའི་དྲི་མཉང་སྒྲུབ་གཞིའི་གཤིས་ལ་མེད་ཀྱང་གློ་བུར་འགྲུལ་པས་བསྐྱེད་པའི་དྲི་མ་གཟུང་འཛིན་གྱི་ཆོས་རྣམས་ཡིན་ཅིང། དེ་སྒྲུབས་པའི་འབྲས་བུ་གཉིས་སྣང་གཟུང་འཛིན་གྱི་དྲི་མ་མཐའ་དག་དང་བྲལ་

(4) Aspiration for unmistaken practice on that path
This has two parts: theory and practice.

a. The theory to understand

7. *The ground of refining is mind itself, the unity of clarity-emptiness.*
The refiner is the great vajra yoga of mahāmudrā.
It refines the object, the stains of incidental delusion.
May I actualize the refined result, stainless dharmakāya.

The ground upon which the stains of samsaric delusion are **refined** was taught by Master Nāgārjuna:

> That very seed that becomes the constituent
> is asserted to be the basis of all qualities.
> Buddhahood will be attained
> through its gradual refinement.[22]

This and endless scriptures speak of the constituent or the buddha nature or the vajra of mind itself. These refer to that which is characterized by **the unity of clarity** and **emptiness**—clarity that is unimpeded intrinsic nature while empty of a basis or root essence. The method for **refining** the stains that accrue to it is presented here from **the great vajra yoga of mahāmudrā** in the convenient instruction system of the great chariot of the unequaled Dakpo Kagyü. The stains that are to be **refined** don't actually exist in the fundamental disposition (*gshis*) of the ground of refinement. However, **stains** arise from **incidental delusions**, producing all phenomena of dualistic subject–object clinging. We aspire to attain the **result of**

བའི་གཉིས་མེད་ཡེ་ཤེས་ཀྱི་ཚོས་སྐུ་མངོན་སུམ་དུ་འགྱུར་བར་མཛད་
ཅིག་ཅེས་པའོ། །ཚོས་སྐུ་དེའང་རང་བཞིན་རྣམ་དག་ལ་གློ་བུར་གྱི་
དྲི་མའང་དག་པས་དག་པ་གཉིས་ལྡན་ནི་སྦྱངས་པ་ཚོས་སྐུའམ་ངོ་
བོ་ཉིད་སྐུ་དང། ཀུན་གཞི། ཁོན་ཡིད། རྒྱ་ཡིད། སྒོ་ལྷའི་རྣམ་ཤེས་
རྣམས་ཡོངས་སུ་དག་ཅིང་གནས་ལྡན་པ་ནི་མཁྱེན་པ་གཉིས་ལྡན་
ཀྱི་ཡེ་ཤེས་རྟོགས་པ་ཚོས་སྐུའམ་ཡེ་ཤེས་ཀྱི་སྐུ་སྟེ་སྦྱངས་རྟོགས་ཀྱི་
སྐུ་གཉིས་དབྱེར་མེད་པ་ནི་ཚོས་སྐུ་ཡོངས་སུ་རྫོགས་པ་ཡིན་ལ། ཕྱི
མ་ལ་དག་བྱ་རྣམ་ཤེས་དེ་རྣམས་ཀྱི་རིམ་པས་མེ་ལོང། མཉམ་ཉིད།
སོར་རྟོག་བྱ་གྱུབ་སྟེ་ཡེ་ཤེས་བཞི་དང་སྐུ་གསུམ་དུ་དབྱེ་བའོ། །

གཉིས་པ་སྒོམ་དོན་ལག་ཏु་ལེན་པའི་སྒོན་ལམ་ལ། བསྟན། བཤད
གཉིས་ལས། དང་པོ་མདོར་བསྟན་པ་ནི།

གཞི་ལ་སྒོ་འདོགས་ཆོད་པ་ལྟ་བའི་གདེང། །དེ་ལ་མ་ཡིངས་སྐྱོང་བ
སྒོམ་པའི་གནད། །སྒོམ་དོན་ཀུན་ལ་ཚལ་སྒྱོང་སྒྱོད་པའི་མཆོག །ལྟ
སྒོམ་སྒྱོད་པའི་གདེང་དང་ལྡན་པར་མཛོག །ཅེས་གསུངས་ཏེ།

refinement, the **actualization** of the **dharmakāya** of nondual timeless awareness, **free of all stains** of dualistic appearance.

The purification (*dag pa*) of incidental stains that accrue to the totally pure intrinsic nature of the dharmakāya leads to having twofold purity (*dag pa gnyis ldan*). That is the abandonment dharmakāya or the svabhāvakāya. The fundamental transformation (*gnas gyur*) from the complete purification of the all-base, afflicted mentality, sixth mental consciousness, and the consciousnesses of the five organs leads to the realized timeless awareness with twofold knowledge (*mkhyen pa gnyis ldan*), which is the dharmakāya or jñānakāya. The inseparability of the two kāyas of abandonment and realization is the completely perfect dharmakāya. Regarding the latter, the consciousnesses that are to be purified are, in order, categorized into the four timeless awarenesses—mirror, equality, discerning, and accomplished—and the three kāyas.

b. The meditation to practice

The aspiration of taking up the practice of meditation has two parts: the presentation and the explanation.

i. Brief presentation

8. *Deep confidence in the view is to sever impositions on the ground.*
The vital point of meditation is to hold that without distraction.
Best conduct is to exercise skill in all meanings of meditation.
May I have deep confidence in view, meditation, and conduct.

ཕྱག་རྒྱ་ཆེན་པོ་ཉམས་སུ་ལེན་པ་ལ་དང་པོར་གཞི་གནས་ལུགས་
ཕྱག་ཆེན་ལ་སྒོ་འདོགས་ཚོད་དེ་ངེས་པ་རྟེད་པ་ལྟ་བའི་གདེང་དང་
ལྡན་ཞིང་ལྟ་བ་དེ་ཉིད་ལ་མཉམ་པར་བཞག་སྟེ་མ་ཡེངས་པར་སྒྲོང་
བ་སྒོམ་པའི་གནད་ལ་མཁས་ཤིང་ཇི་སྐད་གསུངས་པའི་སྒོམ་དོན་
ཀུན་ལ་གོམས་ཤིང་འདྲིས་པར་རྩལ་སྒྲོང་པས་ནི་བོགས་ཐུར་དུ་ཐོན་
པར་འགྱུར་བས་སྒྲོང་པའི་མཚོག་ཏུ་གྱུར་པ་སྟེ། ལྟ་སྒོམ་སྒྲོང་པའི
གནད་དེ་དག་ཚོག་ཙམ་དུ་མ་ཡིས་པར་རང་རྒྱུད་ལ་མངོན་དུ་གྱུར
པའི་གདེང་དང་ལྡན་པར་ཤོག་ཅིག་ཅེས་པའོ།།

གཉིས་པ་རྒྱས་པར་ཕྱི་སྟེ་སྒོམ་པ་ལ་གསུམ། ལྟ་བའི་སྒོ་འདོགས
བཅད། སྒོམ་པས་ཉམས་སུ་བླང་ས། སྒྲོང་པས་མཐར་དབྱུང་བའོ།
།དང་པོ་ལའང་མདོར་བསྟན་པ་དང། རྒྱས་པར་ཕྱི་བ་གཉིས་ལས།
དང་པོ་ཁ་མདོར་བསྟན་པ་ཀ། ནི།

ཆོས་རྣམས་ཐམས་ཅད་སེམས་ཀྱི་རྣམ་འཕྲུལ་ཏེ། །སེམས་ནི་སེམས
མེད་སེམས་ཀྱི་ངོ་བོས་སྟོང། །སྟོང་ཞིང་མ་འགགས་ཅིར་ཡང་སྣང་བ
སྟེ། །ལེགས་པར་བརྟགས་ནས་གཞི་རྩ་ཆོད་པར་ཤོག །

ཅེས་གསུངས་ཏེ། ཚོག་ཀྱང་དང་པོས་སྣང་བ་ཐམས་ཅད་སེམས
ཀྱི་རྣམ་འཕྲུལ་དུ་ཐག་བཅད། གཉིས་པས་སེམས་རང་བཞིན་མེད

In the practice of mahāmudrā, first you must **sever impositions on the ground** or abiding nature of mahāmudrā. In finding such certainty, you gain **deep confidence in the view.** Then to rest in equipoise in that view itself, **holding it without distraction**, you become skilled in the **vital point of meditation. Exercising skill** by getting acquainted and familiar with all the **meanings of meditation** just as they were taught quickly enhances [the experience], leading to the **best conduct.** We aspire to have the **deep confidence** of actualizing the vital points of **view, meditation, and conduct** in the mindstream and not just in words.

ii. Extensive analysis
This explains three parts in the aspiration here: severing superimpositions of the view, practicing through meditation, and consummating through conduct.

A) Severing superimpositions of the view
This has two parts: a brief presentation and an extensive explanation.

1) Brief presentation

9. *All phenomena are projections of the mind.*
As for mind, there is no mind—it is empty of an essence.
But, while empty, it appears freely as anything at all.
Examining this thoroughly, may I sever its base and roots.

The first line establishes that all appearing **phenomena** are the **projections of mind.** The second ascertains that the **mind** has **no** intrinsic nature. The third shows that **emptiness** and

པར་གཏན་ལ་ཕབ། གསུམ་པས་སྟོང་དང་རྟེན་འབྲེལ་ཟུང་འཇུག་མི་འགལ་བར་བསྟན། བཞི་པས་དེ་ལྟར་སོར་རྟོག་གི་ཤེས་རབ་ཀྱིས་བརྟགས་པས་གཞིའི་དོན་ལ་སྒོ་འདོགས་གཅོད་དགོས་པ་ལ་སྒོན་པའོ།།

གཉིས་པ་དེ་རྒྱས་པར་ཕྱི་བ་ལའང་དེ་ལྟར་བཞི་ལས། དང་པོ་སྟང་བ་སེམས་སུ་ཐག་བཅད་པ་ནི།

ཡོད་མ་ཐོང་བའི་རང་སྟང་ཡུལ་དུ་འཁྱལ། །མ་རིག་དབང་གིས་རང་རིག་བདག་དུ་འཁྱལ། །གཉིས་འཛིན་དབང་གིས་སྲིད་པའི་གློང་དུ་འཁྱམས། །མ་རིག་འཁྱལ་པའི་ཚད་དར་ཆོད་པར་ཤོག

།ཅེས་གསུངས་ཏེ། འོད་གསལ་སེམས་ཀྱི་རྩོ་ཇེ་ཅོ་བོ་སྟོང་ཞིང་རང་བཞིན་གསལ་བས་ཆུམ་པ་འགག་མེད་དུ་ཤར་བ་ཉིད་རང་དང་དུས་ལྡན་ཕྱི་མེད་པར་ལྷན་ཅིག་སྐྱེས་པའི་མ་རིག་པ་གསེར་དང་གཡའ་ལྟ་བུའི་དྲི་མས་བསྒྲིབས་ཏེ། རང་གི་ངོ་བོ་རང་ཚུལ་ཀྱིས་མ་རིག་པས་འདུ་བྱེད་ཀྱི་ཡིད་གཡོས། ཆུམ་ཤེས་སྐྱེས་ཏེ་ཡུལ་དང་འཛིན་པ་གཉིས་སུ་སྣང་བ་རང་གིས་རང་ལ་གཏད་ཅིང་བཟུང་སྟེ་འཁྱལ་བའི་བག་ཆགས་ཇི་ཆེར་ཐུས་ནས་རྒྱན་འཕྲོལ་བཅུ་གཉིས་ཀྱིས་བྱ་དང་སྒོ་ང་ལྟར་འགོར་བ་སྟེ། དག་པའི་སེམས་ཉིད་ཀྱི་རང་གཤིས་ལ་ཡེ་ནས་ཡོད་མ་ཐོང་བའི་རང་ཚུལ་ལས་ཉེ་བར་སྟང་བའི་རང་བཞིན་གསལ་བའི་ཆ་ལ་དེ་ལྟར་དུ་མ་རྟོགས་པས་རང་གི་རང་ལ་ཕྱི་དོན་ཡུལ་གཞན་དུ་བཟུང་སྟེ་འཁྱལ་ཞིང། མ་རིག་པའི་དབང་

interdependence are a unity and not a contradiction. The fourth makes the aspiration that it is necessary to **sever** superimpositions by **examining** with discriminating wisdom.

2) Extensive explanation
The first of four parts:

a) Establishing that all appearances are the projections of mind

10. *Mind's displays that never existed are mistaken for objects.*
Innate awareness is ignorantly mistaken for a self.
We wander in the expanse of existence by such dualism.
May I get to the bottom of delusional mistakes.

The vajra mind of lucid clarity is empty in essence, lucid by nature, and arises unimpededly in form. Innate ignorance arises simultaneously, neither before nor after. Like dross on gold, it is obscured by stains. Its dynamic energy is ignorant of its own essence, so a formative cognition stirs. Consciousness is born, and then the dualistic perception that fixates on object and subject. One regards oneself and grasps that [as an object]. The habitual pattern of delusion increases more and more and one circles around in the twelve links of interdependence like the chicken and the egg.

The innate dynamic energy (*rang rtsal*) of the innate disposition (*rang gshis*) of pure **mind** itself **that never existed displays** itself as subjective appearance (*nye bar snang ba*). Through not realizing that appearance as the clarity aspect of your intrinsic nature, you subjectively grasp yourself as an external **object**—an other—and are thus **mistaken**. Under

གཞན་རང་རིག་གཞི་མེད་ཙ་བླལ་དུ་མ་རྟོགས་པར་ཁོན་མོངས་པའི་
ཡིད་ཀྱིས་ཡུལ་འཛིན་པ་པོ་ངའི་སྣམ་དུ་ངོ་བོ་སྟོང་པའི་ཚ་ལ་བདག་
ཏུ་རྟོག་སྟེ་འཁྱལ་ནས། བདག་གཞན་གཉིས་སྣང་གཟུང་འཛིན་གྱི་
རྟོག་པས་ཆགས་སྡང་རྨོངས་གསུམ་རྒྱས། དེས་ལས་བསགས་ཏེ་དེའི་
དབང་གིས་སྲིད་གསུམ་འགོར་བའི་གློང་དུ་འཁྱམས་པ་ཡིན་པས་
ན་གཟུང་འཛིན་གཉིས་བསྟེན་ཀྱི་ཆོས་ཐམས་ཅད་འཁྱལ་བ་ཁོ་ན་
ཡིན་ལ་འཁྱལ་གཞིའང་སེམས་ཡིན་པས། སེམས་ལས་ཡོགས་སུ་རྒྱལ་
ཙམ་མ་གྱུར་སྟེ། དཔེ་སྟེགས་ཀྱི་སྟོར་བས་ནམ་མཁའ་ལ་རྒྱ་གླང་སྣང་
བ་ལྟ་བུའོ། །དེས་ན་མ་རིག་པའི་དབང་གིས་ཇི་ལྟར་འཁྱལ་ཚུལ
མ་ཤེས་ན་འཁྱལ་བར་མི་མཐོང་ཞིང། དེ་མ་མཐོང་ན་སྟོང་དུ་མི
བཏུབ་པའི་ཕྱིར་དེའི་གནད་རྩད་དར་ཆོད་པར་ཤོག་ཅིག་ཅེས་པའོ།
།དེ་ལྟར་ཐོག་མེད་ནས་ཙ་འཛས་ཀྱི་བག་ཆགས་ཁོམས་ཆེས་པས
འགོར་བའི་ཆོས་དངོས་སྣང་རགས་པ་འདི་རྣམས་སེམས་ཀྱི་གནས
ཚུལ་དང་ཤིན་ཏུ་འགལ་བ་ལྟར་འདུག་པ་འདི་སེམས་སུ་གཏན་ལ
ཕེབས་ན། ཕ་བ་རྣམ་བྱང་གི་ཆོས་རྣམས་ནི་སེམས་ཀྱི་གནས་ཚུལ
དང་ཇེས་སུ་མཐུན་པས་བདེ་བླག་ཏུ་ཤེས་པའི་ཕྱིར་ཤུགས་ལ་བསྟན
པ་སྟེ། དེས་ན་རྣམ་བྱང་གི་ཆོས་ཐམས་ཅད་ཀྱང་དག་པའི་སེམས
ཀྱི་རང་བཞིན་ལས་མ་འདས་ཏེ། དྲི་བཅས་ཀྱི་སྐབས་སུ་སེམས་ཡིད
རྣམ་ཤེས་གསུམ་པོ་དྲི་བླལ་ཀྱི་ཚ་སྐུ་གསུམ་དུ་རྣམ་པར་འཇོག་
པའི་ཕྱིར། ལམ་ཀྱི་སྐབས་སྒྲུབ་བྱའི་དྲི་མ་ཇི་སྲིད་ཏུ་སོང་བཞིན་དག
པའི་སེམས་ལ་གནས་པའི་ཡོན་ཏན་ཇི་གསལ་དུ་འགྱུར་ཞིང། དྲི
མ་ཐམས་ཅད་དག་ཚེ་གཞིའི་ཡོན་ཏན་ཐམས་ཅད་སྣང་བ་རྒྱུད་བླ

the influence of this **ignorance**, the afflicted mentation that does not realize that **innate awareness** (*rang rig*) is groundless and rootless thinks that the one who subjectively grasps objects is "I" and conceives of the empty essence aspect as **a self**, again being **mistaken**. With such concepts of **dualistic** subject–object appearances of self and other, the three afflictions of attraction, aversion, and neutral stupidity are born. With that, you accumulate karma and under its power you become a **wanderer in the expanse** of the three cyclic **existences**. Therefore, all phenomena included in subject–object dualism are only delusion. But the basis of delusion is mind. Apart from the mind, not a single atom is established as existent. For instance, it is like the magical appearances of horses and elephants in the sky produced by applying mantra. Therefore if, under the power of **ignorance**, you do not understand the way you are **mistakenly deluded**, then you do not see it as delusion. Since you cannot eliminate what you cannot see, we aspire to **get to the bottom** of that vital point.

In that way, the powerful conditioning of habitual patterns of reification since beginningless time have caused these coarse manifest appearances of samsaric phenomena, which are like the total opposite of the mind's way of abiding. When these are ascertained as mind, the subtle totally pure phenomena which *are* consistent with the abiding nature of mind are easy to understand, so that is revealed implicitly. Therefore, all perfectly pure phenomena do not transcend the intrinsic nature of the pure mind. At the time of having stains, there is the triad of all-ground, afflicted mentation, and consciousness.[23] From the stainless aspect, these are classified as the three kāyas. Therefore, at the time of the path, as the stains that are to be refined grow weaker, the qualities that dwell

མ་ལས་གསུངས་པ་ལྟར་རོ། །རྒྱུ་མཚན་འདིས་གདུལ་བྱའི་ཤེས་རྒྱུད་
དག་རིམ་གྱིས་སངས་རྒྱས་སྐུ་གསུམ་མཐོང་བའང་ཤེས་པར་བྱའོ། །

གཉིས་པ་སེམས་རང་བཞིན་མེད་པར་གཏན་ལ་འབེབས་པ་ལ·
གཉིས། ཡོད་མེད་དང། ཡིན་མིན་གྱི་མཐའ་སྤོང་བའོ། །དང་པོ་ཡོད·
མེད་ཀྱི་མཐའ་སྤོང་བ་ཀ། ནི།

ཡོད་པ་མ་ཡིན་རྒྱལ་བས་ཀྱང་མ་གཟིགས། །མེད་པ་མ་ཡིན་འགོར·
འདས་ཀུན་ཀྱི་གཞི། །འགལ་འདུ་མ་ཡིན་ཟུང་འཇུག་དབུ་མའི་ལམ།
།མཐའ་བྲལ་སེམས་ཀྱི་ཆོས་ཉིད་རྟོགས་པར་ཤོག

།ཅི་གསུངས་ཏེ། འགོར་འདས་ཐམས་ཅད་སེམས་ཡིན་ན་སེམས་དེ·
བདེན་གྱབ་ཏུ་ཡོད་དམ་ཞེ་ན། བདེན་གྱབ་ཏུ་ཡོད་པ་ལྟ་ཅི་སྟོས·
བདེན་བརྫུན་གང་གི་ཕྱོགས་དོར་ཡང་ཡོད་པ་མ་ཡིན་ཏེ། རྒྱལ་བ·
ཐམས་ཅད་མཁྱེན་པའི་ཡེ་ཤེས་ཀྱིས་ཀྱང་མ་གཟིགས་མི་གཟིགས·
གཟིགས་པར་མི་འགྱུར་གསུངས་པའི་ཕྱིར། བོ་ན་ཅང་མེད་བེམ་སྟོང·
ནམ་མཁའ་ལྟ་བུར་བལྟའམ་ཞེ་ན། དེ་ལྟར་དུ་འང་མི་བལྟ་སྟེ་སེམས·
རང་བཞིན་གྱིས་དག་པའི་ཁམས་དེ་མེད་ན་འགོར་འདས་ཀྱི་སྣང·
བ་ཀུན་ཇི་བ་ཙམ་དུ་འང་འཕྲུང་མི་རིགས་པའི་ཕྱིར་མེད་པའང་མ·
ཡིན་ཏེ། འགོར་བར་འཕྲུལ་གཞི་དང་ཆུང་འདས་སུ་ཞོལ་གཞི་སྟེ·
འགོར་འདས་ཀུན་ཀྱི་གཞི་ཡིན་པའི་ཕྱིར་སྟོང་ཉིད་དཔོན་གྱུ་ཞབས་ཀྱིས།

in the pure mind grow clearer. When all stains are purified, all the qualities of the ground manifest, as is taught in the *Mahāyāna Highest Continuum*.[24] You should understand that it is for this reason that as the disciples' mindstreams are gradually purified, they [gradually] see the three kāyas of a buddha.

b) Ascertaining that mind has no intrinsic existence
This has two parts: abandoning extremes of existence/nonexistence and being/nonbeing.

i) Avoiding extremes of existence and nonexistence

11. *It does not exist; even the victors don't see it.*
It doesn't not exist; it's the basis of all samsara and nirvana.
No contradiction; it's the middle way of unity.
May I realize mind's true nature without extremes.

If the whole of samsara and nirvana is the mind, wouldn't that mind be established as truly existing? Never mind being established as truly existent, even discard any sort of validity or falsity, for **it does not exist**. As it says, all **the victors** with their timeless awareness that knows all **don't see it**, have not seen it, and will not see it. Well then, can we view it as being like space, with nothing at all but empty matter? Don't look at it that way either. Because if it were not for mind's naturally pure constituent,[25] it would be unreasonable for all the appearances of samsara and nirvana to arise even conventionally. So **it doesn't not exist**, because **it is the basis of all samsara and nirvana**—the basis of delusion in samsara and the basis of liberation in nirvana. Master Nāgārjuna said,

།བསམ་ཡོད་ནི་ལས་བྱས་པས། །ས་ལ་ལྷམ་དག་མཛོང་བར་འགྱུར། །བསམ་མེད་ནི་ལས་བྱང་ཀྱང། །ངལ་བ་འབའ་ཞིག་སྐྱེད་པར་ཟད། །ཅེས་གསུངས་སོ། །འོ་ན་གཞི་གཅིག་ལ་ཡོད་མེད་གཉིས་འགལ་ལོ་ཞེ་ན། འགལ་བ་འདུ་བའང་ཡིན་ཏེ་ཡོད་མེད་གཉིས་བཀག་པ་ལས་བསྟན་པ་མ་ཡིན་པའི་ཕྱིར། དེས་ན་ཡོད་མེད་སྟོང་མི་སྟོང་སོགས་གང་དུའང་བཙོད་མི་ནུས་ལ་གང་དུའང་མི་གནས་ཤིང་མཐའ་བྲལ་དེ་ལ་ཟུང་འཇུག་རབ་ཏུ་མི་གནས་པའི་དབུ་མའི་ལམ་ཞེས་ཐ་སྙད་ཅམ་དུ་གདགས་པ་ཡིན་པས་དེ་ལྟ་བུའི་མཐའ་བྲལ་སེམས་ཀྱི་ཆོས་ཉིད་སྒོས་པ་ཀུན་བྲལ་ཉིད་རྟོགས་པར་ཤོག་ཅེས་པའོ། །

གཉིས་པ་ཡིན་མིན་ཀྱི་མཐའ་སྟོང་བ་ནི།

འདི་ཡིན་ཞེས་པ་གང་གིས་མཚོན་པ་མེད། །འདི་མིན་ཞེས་བྱ་གང་གིས་བཀག་པ་མེད། །བློ་ལས་འདས་པའི་ཆོས་ཉིད་འདུས་མ་བྱས། །ཡང་དག་དོན་ཀྱི་མཐའ་ནི་ངེས་པར་ཤོག

།ཅེས་གསུངས་ཏེ། འདིའི་དོན་སྤར་ཡོད་མེད་ཀྱི་མཐའ་བཀག་པས་ཀྱང་ཤེས་མོད། རང་བཞིན་མཐའ་བྲལ་དེ་ལ་སྟོང་ཉིད་སྐྱེ་མེད་བདེ་ཆེན་ཡེ་ཤེས་སོགས་མིང་སྐྱན་དགོས་འདི་ལྟར་ཡིན་ནོ་ཞེས་པ་དཔེ་ཚོག་གང་གིས་ཀྱང་མཚོན་པ་མེད་ཅིང། འདི་ནི་འདི་ལྟར་མིན་ནོ་མེད་དོ་ཞེས་བྱ་བའི་དཔེ་ཚོག་གང་གིས་ཀྱང་བཀག་པ་བྱར་མེད་དེ་མཚོན་བྱའི་ཆོས་དང་དགག་བསྟན་ཀྱི་གཞི་མ་གྲུབ་ཅིང་བློའི་སྤྱོད་ཡུལ་ལས་འདས་པའི་ཕྱིར་སྒྲས་ཀྱང་བཙོད་མི་ནུས་ཏེ།

If the constituent is present,
with effort you will see pure gold.
Without the constituent,
effort generates nothing but affliction.[26]

But isn't it a contradiction for a single basis to be both existent and nonexistent? It is an internal **contradiction** because it did not establish [something] by refuting both existence and nonexistence. Therefore, you cannot say anything at all, such as existence, nonexistence, empty, not empty, and so forth, and since there is no traction anywhere, it is free of extremes—so **it is** called the "**middle way** path **of** total nonabiding **unity.**"[27] Since that is a mere designation, we aspire to **realize** the **true nature** of **mind without extremes**,[28] actual freedom from all embellishment.

ii) Avoiding extremes of being and nonbeing

12. *To say "this is" doesn't indicate anything.*
To say "this is not" doesn't refute anything.
Unformed true nature defies the intellect.
May I gain certainty in the range of genuine reality.

Certainly you can comprehend the meaning here through the previous refutation of the extremes of existence and nonexistence. There are many sweet-sounding names for that intrinsic nature free of extremes that you can use **to say** "**it is** like **this**," such as "emptiness," "unborn," "great bliss," "timeless awareness," and so forth. But these metaphorical words **do not indicate anything**. **To say** "**this is not** like this" and use metaphorical words also **does not refute anything**. That is because

མདོ་ལས། ཡང་དག་ཉིད་དུ་གཉིས་མེད་དེ། །དེ་ནི་སྟོས་པ་མེད་པ་
ཡིན། །འཇམ་དཔལ་གྱིས་ནི་ཡང་དག་དྲིས། །རྒྱལ་བའི་སྲས་པོ་མི་
སྐྱ་བཞུགས། །ཞེས་འབྱུང་བའི་ཕྱིར་བློ་འདས་དེ་ནི་ཆོས་ཐམས་ཅད་
ཀྱི་ཆོས་ཉིད་ཡིན་ཅིང་འདུས་མ་བྱས་པའི་ཕྱིར་སྟོས་པའི་རྒྱུན་གང་
གིས་ཀྱང་འགྱུར་བ་མེད་པའི་དེ་བཞིན་ཉིད་དང། མཚན་མ་མེད་པ
དང། དོན་དམ་དང། ཆོས་དབྱིངས་དང། ཡང་དག་པའི་མཐའ་ཞེས
རྣམ་གྲངས་དུ་མས་བསྟན་པའི་གནས་ལུགས་སྟོང་ཉིད་ཀྱི་དོན་ནི
སོམ་ཉི་མེད་པའི་ངེས་པ་རྟེད་པར་མཛོག་ཅིག་ཅེས་པའོ། །འདིར་ཀུན
མཁྱེན་གྱི་ཏུའི་གསུང་སྨྲིང་པོར་བསྟུས་ཏེ་གོ་སྒྲ་བར་བཀོད་པ་ཡིན
ལ། འདིའི་དོན་མཁས་མེད་དགས་པོའི་གསུང་གསང་གིས་གསལ
བར་འཚད་དུའང་ཡོད་དོ། །

གསུམ་པ་སྟོང་དང་རྟེན་འབྱུང་ཟུང་འཇུག་མི་འགལ་བ་ནི།

འདི་ཉིད་མ་རྟོགས་འགོར་བའི་རྒྱ་མཚོར་འགོར། །འདི་ཉིད་རྟོགས
ན་སངས་རྒྱས་གཞན་ན་མེད། །ཐམས་ཅད་འདི་ཡིན་འདི་མིན་གང
ཡང་མེད། །ཆོས་ཉིད་ཀུན་གཞིའི་མཚང་ནི་རིག་པར་མཛོག

།ཅེས་གསུངས་ཏེ། དེས་ན་གནས་ལུགས་སེམས་ཀྱི་གསང་འདི་ཉིད
མ་རྟོགས་པ་ལས་ལུགས་འབྱུང་རྟེན་བྱེལ་ཀྱིས་འགོར་བའི་རྒྱ་མཚོར

the phenomena that are indicated and the bases of refutation and affirmation are not established, so it **defies** the realm of **the intellect**. It cannot even be expressed by sound. It says in a sutra:

> The nonduality of the genuine state
> is without embellishment.
> When Mañjuśrī inquired about it,
> the bodhisattva sat silently.[29]

Therefore it transcends the intellect because it is the **true nature** (*dharmatā*) of all phenomena (*dharma*) and therefore **is unformed**, not subject to any conditions of embellishment. Unchanging suchness, no characteristics, ultimate reality, realm of phenomena, **range of genuine reality**—these many synonyms are used to present the abiding nature, the meaning of emptiness. We aspire to gain certainty without doubt.

Here, all-knowing Situ[30] has presented an abridged essence of his teachings for easy comprehension. Its meaning was also clearly explicated in the secret teachings of the Unequalled Dakpo (Gampopa).

c) The unity of emptiness and interdependence is not contradictory

13. *Not to realize this is to flounder in samsara's ocean.*
To realize it is nothing other than buddhahood.
Being all, "this is it" and "this is not it" mean nothing at all.
May I awaken to the true nature hidden in the all-ground.

Not to realize this, the abiding nature, the secret of the mind, is to **flounder in the ocean of samsara** through

འགོར་བ་ཡིན་ལ། འདི་ཁྱོད་རྟོགས་ན་ལུགས་སྟོག་རྒྱན་འཕེལ་གྱིས་ འཚང་རྒྱ་བ་ཡིན་པས་ཐར་རྒྱས་དེའང་གནས་ལུགས་ཀྱི་དོན་ འདི་ལས་གཞན་བོགས་ཤིག་ན་མེད་ཅིང། གནས་ལུགས་དེ་བཞིན་ ཁྱོད་ཐར་རྒྱས་ཀྱི་རང་བཞིན་འདིས་ཆོས་ཐམས་ཅད་ལ་ཡེ་ནས་ ཁྱབ་པས་ཐམས་ཅད་འདི་ཡིན་ལ། འདི་མིན་པའི་ཆོས་ཤིག་གང་དུ་ བཙལ་ཡང་རྙེད་པ་མེད་དེ། ཆོས་རྣམས་རྟེན་འབྱུང་ཡིན་པའི་རྒྱུན་ མཚན་ཀྱིས་སྟོང་ཁྱད་དུ་གོ་བར་ནུས་ཏེ་སྟོང་ཁྱད་མ་ཡིན་ན་རྟེན་ འབྱུང་མི་རུང་བའི་ཕྱིར། ཀླུ་སྒྲུབ་ཞབས་ཀྱིས། རྟེན་ཅིང་འབྲེལ་འབྱུང་ མ་ཡིན་པའི། ।ཆོས་འགའ་ཡོད་པ་མ་ཡིན་ལ། ।འདི་ཕྱིར་སྟོང་ཁྱད་ མ་ཡིན་པའི། ।ཆོས་འགར་ཡོད་པ་མ་ཡིན་ནོ། ।ཞེས་སོགས་རྒྱ་ཆེར་ གསུངས་པ་ལྟར་སྣང་བ་རྟེན་འབྱུང་གི་ངོ་བོ་སྟོང་པ་ཁྱད་ཀྱི་ཕྱིར་ ཟུང་དུ་འཇུག་པ་སྟེ། དེ་ལྟར་ཆོས་ཐམས་ཅད་ཀྱི་ཆོས་ཁྱད་དེ་བཞིན་ ཁྱད་ཀུན་གཞི་ངང་ལུགས་དགེ་བ་ཞེས་བྱ་བའི་གནད་མཚང་ཇི་ལྟ་ བ་བཞིན་དུ་ནི་རིག་པར་ཤོག་ཅིག་ཅེས་པའོ། ।

བཞི་པ་དེ་ལྟར་བརྟགས་པས་གཞི་རྩ་ཆོད་པར་སྨོན་པ་ནི།

སྣང་ཡང་ཞེམས་ལ་སྟོང་ཡང་ཞེམས་ཡིན་ཏེ། ।རྟོགས་ཀྱང་ཞེམས་ལ་ འབྱུལ་ཡང་རང་གི་ཞེམས། ।རྒྱུས་ཀྱང་ཞེམས་ལ་འགག་ཀྱང་ཞེམས་ ཡིན་པས། ।སྨོ་འདོགས་ཐམས་ཅད་ཞེམས་ལ་ཆོད་པར་ཤོག

interdependent origination operating in progressive order. **To realize it** is **buddhahood** due to interdependent origination operating in reverse order. Therefore, that buddhahood is **nothing other than** this very meaning of the abiding nature. The abiding nature, suchness, the intrinsic nature of a buddha, pervades all phenomena since forever. Therefore, **all is this**. However much you search, you cannot find a single phenomenon that **is not this**. All phenomena are interdependently arisen. For that reason, we can understand emptiness; for if there were no emptiness, interdependent origination would make no sense. Noble Nāgārjuna said,

> There do not exist any phenomena
> that do not originate interdependently.
> Therefore, there do not exist any phenomena
> that are not emptiness.[31]

Likewise, it is explained at length that since emptiness is the essence of the interdependent origination of appearance, they are a unified pair. In this way, the **true nature** of all phenomena, the suchness, abides intrinsically within **the all-ground** and is called "virtue." We aspire to **awaken to** this inner **hidden nature** just as it is.

d) The aspiration to cut through the basic root by such examination

14. *As appearance is mind, so too emptiness is mind.*
As realization is mind, delusion is also one's mind.
As birth is mind, so is cessation the mind.
May I sever all the impositions of mind.

།ཅིས་གསུངས་ཏེ། མངོར་ན་སྣང་སྲིད་རྟོག་འགྲུལ་གྱི་འགག་རྩམས་
སྟར་སྨོས་པའི་རྒྱུན་མཚན་དེ་དག་ཇིས་པའི་སྒོ་ནས་རང་བཞིན་
མེད་པར་གཏན་ལ་ཕབ་པ་གནས་ལུགས་ཀྱི་སྒོ་འདོགས་ཐམས་ཅད་
སེམས་ལ་ཚོད་པར་ཤོག་ཅེས་སམ། མངོར་ན་ཀུན་རྫོབ་ཏུ་སྣང་བ་
ཡང་སེམས་ཀྱི་འཁྲུལ་བ་ཡིན་ལ་དོན་དམ་སྟོང་པ་ཡང་སེམས་ཀྱི་
གནས་ལུགས་ཡིན་ཏེ། དེ་ཉིད་རྟོགས་ནས་ས་ཐམས་རྒྱས་ཀྱང་དག་པའི་
སེམས་ཉིད་ཡིན་ལ་འཁྲུལ་ཏེ་འཁོར་བར་འཁྱམས་ན་ཡང། རང་གི་
མ་དག་པའི་སེམས་སྣང་ཡིན་པའི་ཕྱིར་དེས་ན་སེམས་རྒྱུད་མར་སྐྱེས་
ཏེ་སྲིད་པར་འཁྱམས་ཀྱང་སེམས་ཡིན་ལ་ས་སོར་བརྒྱགས་འགོག
གིས་འགགས་ཏེ་ཞི་བ་ཐོབ་ཀྱང་སེམས་ཡིན་པས་བདེན་གཉིས
འཁོར་འདས་སྲིད་ཞི་སོགས་ཐམས་ཅད་སེམས་དྲི་བཅས་དྲི་མེད
གཉིས་ལས་མ་འདས་ཤིང། དེའང་སྟོང་པ་གཞི་མེད་ཆ་བྲལ་མཐའ
གང་དུའང་མི་གནས་པས་བློ་འདས་ཉིད་དུ་ངེས་པའི་སྒོ་འདོགས
ཐམས་ཅད་སེམས་ལ་ཚོད་ནས་དེ་ཉིད་མངོན་དུ་བྱ་ཐབས་གཟུང
འཛིན་གྱི་དྲི་མ་སྤྱོང་ཕྱིར་སྨོན་པ་ཉམས་ལེན་ལ་འབད་པར་ཤོག
ཅེས་ལྟ་བ་ལ་ངེས་པ་ཆེད་ནས་སྨོན་པ་ལ་འཇུག་པར་མཚམས་སྦྱར
བ་སྟེ། རྒྱུད་ལས། རིན་ཆེན་སེམས་ལས་ཕྱིར་ཡུར་པའི། །ས་ངེས་རྒྱས
མེད་ཅིང་སེམས་ཅན་མེད། །ཅེས་དང། ཀུན་པའི་ཕྱི་མེས་ས་ར་ཏ
པས།

In brief, may we cut through all superimpositions of appearance and emptiness, realization and delusion, birth and cessation, imposed on the abiding nature by ascertaining their lack of intrinsic nature and by gaining the certainty in the reasons presented previously.

Or, in brief, **as** conventional **appearance is** also the delusion of the **mind, so too** the **emptiness** of ultimate reality **is mind**'s abiding nature. Once there is **realization** of that very truth, even buddha is pure **mind** itself. **As** that is [obscured by] **delusion,** one wanders in cyclic existence. However, since that is the appearance of **one's** impure **mind**, the mental continuum takes **birth** in a mother and wanders in existence. However, this is also mind and may be stopped by the **cessation** from discriminating analysis and peace gained, which too **is mind**. Therefore all designations such as the two truths, samsara and nirvana, existence and peace, and so forth do not transcend the two aspects of stained or stainless mind. Baseless and rootless emptiness does not exist in any extreme whatsoever. With the certitude in that state beyond intellect, **may I sever all the superimpositions** [by realizing them as] the **mind**. Since the method to manifest that is to purify the stains of subject–object dualism, we aspire to endeavor in the practice of meditation. This is the juncture of entering into meditation once one has gained certainty in the view. It says in a tantra:

> Outside of the precious mind
> there are no buddhas or sentient beings.[32]

There are vast teachings on this, such as by our ancestor, the adept Saraha:

སེམས་ཉིད་གཅིག་པུ་ཀུན་གྱི་ས་བོན་ཏེ། །གང་ལས་སྲིད་དང་མྱང་
ངན་འདས་འཕྲོ་བ། །འདོད་པའི་འཕྲས་བུ་སྟེར་བར་བྱེད་པ་ཡི།
།ཡིན་བཞིན་ནོར་འདྲའི་སེམས་ལ་ཕྱག་འཚལ་ལོ། །ཞེས་སོགས་རྒྱ
ཆེར་གསུངས་པའི་ཕྱིར་རོ། །

གཉིས་པ་སྒོམ་པས་ཉམས་སུ་ལེན་ཚུལ་ལ། བསྟན། བཤད་གཉིས
ལས། དང་པོ་མདོར་བསྟན་པ་ནི།

བློས་བྱས་རྩོལ་བའི་སྒོམ་གྱིས་མ་བསླད་ཅིང། །ཐ་མལ་འདུ་འཛིའི
ཆུང་གིས་མ་བསྐྱོད་པར། །མ་བཅོས་གཤིག་མར་རང་བབས་འཛིག
ཤེས་པའི། །སེམས་དོན་ཉམས་ལེན་མཁས་ཤིང་སྐྱོང་བར་བྱོག

།ཅེས་གསུངས་ཏེ། ཀུན་མཁྱེན་ཞི་ཏུས་འདིའི་ཚོག་རྣང་གཉིས་པ
ཐོག་མར་བྱས་ནི་བཤད་བདེ་བར་གསུངས་པ་ལྟར། དང་པོ་སྒོམ་ལ
འཇུག་པའི་ཚུལ་མཚན་ལྟན་གྱི་བླ་མ་ཚུལ་བཞིན་བསྟེན་པའི་སྐལ
ལྟན་གྱི་སློབ་མ་དེས། ཐོག་མར་ཕྱིམ་དང་དགྱ་གཉིན་ནོར་ཤས་ཆེད
བཀུར་སོགས་འཇིག་རྟེན་ཆོས་བརྒྱད་ལ་ཞེན་པའི་ཆགས་ལྡང་མ
སྤངས་ནས་ཐར་པ་ལྟ་ཅི་སྨོས་མཐོ་རིས་ཀྱང་མི་འཐོབ་པས་སྒོ་གསུམ
འཇིག་རྟེན་ཐ་མལ་པའི་ཐྲོད་པ་འདུ་འཛིའི་ཆུང་གིས་མ་བསྐྱོད

Mind itself is the single seed of all,
from which existence and nirvana emanate.
Homage to mind, like a wish-fulfilling gem
that grants the gift of the desired fruit.[33]

B) How to take into experience through meditation
This has two parts, a brief presentation and an explanation.

1) Brief presentation

15. *Unspoiled by meditation with mind-made effort,*
unmoved by the winds of everyday affairs,
knowing how to fall naturally in the uncontrived innate state;
may I skillfully maintain the practice of mind's meaning.

The all-knowing Situ said that it is better to explain this verse if the second line comes first. In keeping with that, first we will discuss the way to enter into meditation. Those who attend an authentic guru correctly are fortunate disciples. But if right from the start they do not abandon attraction and aversion that clings to a household and the eight worldly concerns—including friend and foe, property and wealth, honor and gain—they will not even attain higher states, let alone emancipation. Therefore, stay in a remote place and practice **unmoved by the winds of everyday affairs** and worldly activities of the three doors. Train with the common, uncommon, and special preliminaries, positively blending them with your very being and not just according to duration of time or accumulation of repetitions. That way, mind will turn toward Dharma, Dharma will become the path, and the

པར་དབེན་པའི་གནས་སུ། ཐུན་མོང་དང་ཐུན་མིན་དང་ཁྱད་པར་
གྱི་སྟོན་འགྲོ་རྣམས་དུས་གྱངས་ཙམ་མིན་པར་རང་རྒྱུད་ལ་འདྲེས་
ཏེས་པ་སྦྱངས་པས་བློ་ཚོས་དང་ཚོས་ལམ་དུ་འགྲོ་ཞིང་ཕྱག་ཆེན་གྱི་
ཡེ་ཤེས་རྩོལ་མེད་དུ་རྒྱུ་བའི་རྟེན་འབྲེལ་ལེགས་པར་བསྒྲིགས་ནས།
བར་དུ་མཁན་པར་འཛིག་ཚུལ་ལས་གནད་ཚུལ་བཞིན་བཅས་ནས་
ཁྱུང་ཙོ་བས་ལ། ཞེམས་གནད་རང་གི་བློ་བྱས་པའི་གསལ་བ་དང་
སྟོང་པ་སོགས་ལེགས་ལེགས་ལྟ་བའི་རྩོལ་བའི་སྒོམ་གྱིས་མ་བསླད་
ཅིང། དཔལ་ས་ར་ཏས། འདི་ལྟར་དུས་གསུམ་རྣམ་པ་ཐམས་ཅད་
དུ། །ཡིད་ལ་བྱར་མེད་མ་བྱལ་གཅུག་མའི་ངང། །དེ་ཉིད་སྒོང་ལ་
སྒོམ་ཞེས་ཐ་སྙད་གདགས། །ཞེས་གསུངས་པ་ལྟར་བཀའ་བརྒྱུད་གོང་
མ་རྣམས་ཀྱི་ཞལ་ནས། འདས་པའི་རྗེས་མི་གཅད། མ་འོངས་པའི་
མདུན་མི་བསུ། ད་ལྟར་གྱི་ཤེས་པ་བཟོ་བཅོས་མེད་པར་རང་བབས་
སུ་འཇོག་གསུངས་པ་ལྟར་མ་བཅོས་གཅུག་མའི་ངང་ལ་རང་བབས་
སུ་འཇོག་ཤེས་པའི་སེམས་དོན་ཁམས་སུ་ལེན་པའི་མན་ངག་གི་
གནད་ལ་མཁས་ཤིང་ཕྱིང་ཚོད་བསལ་བ། གོལ་ས་གཅོད་པ། བོགས་
འདོན་པ་རྣམས་ཀྱང་ཇི་བཞིན་ཤེས་པའི་སྒོ་ནས་འཕྲས་བུའི་ཕྱག་
ཆེན་མངོན་དུ་མ་ཐུར་གྱི་བར་དུ་རྒྱུན་བསྲིངས་ཏེ་སྒྲོང་བར་ནུས་
པའི་སྣལ་པ་དང་ལྡན་པར་ཤོག་ཅེག་ཅེས་པའོ། །ཅི་ཐོག་མ་ཉིད་
ནས་བཟོ་མེད་དུ་སྒྲོང་བ་ཉིད་ལ་འཇུག་གམ་ཞེ་ན། འཇུག་པར་ནུས་
ན་ཆེས་ལེགས་ཤིང་གང་ཟག་གི་དབང་པོའི་རིམ་པས་མ་ནུས་ན།
འཕགས་པ་ཐུས། དམིགས་པ་དག་ལ་བརྟེན་ནས་ནི། ། དམིགས་མེད་
པ་ཉིད་རབ་ཏུ་སྒྲུ། །

interdependent connections are set into motion for the timeless awareness of mahāmudrā to arise effortlessly.

In the middle, (until then), practice clearing away the dead air according to the vital points from the teachings on the way of entering equipoise. For the vital points of mind, remain **unspoiled by meditation with effort** that is like being impressed by **mind-made** clarity and emptiness and so forth, and follow glorious Saraha's teaching:

> In this way, during all the three times,
> maintain the innate state free of mental engagement;
> this is what is meant by the term "meditation."[34]

Just so, the Kagyü masters of the past all said, "Do not get stuck in the past, do not go out to greet the future, fall naturally in the wakefulness of the present moment without artifice or contrivance." Accordingly, **know how to fall naturally in the uncontrived innate state** with **skill** in the vital points of the esoteric instructions concerning the practice of **mind's meaning**. By means of the accurate knowledge of how to eliminate dullness and agitation, cutting off deviations, and employing the enhancements, you continue to **maintain the practice** until the actualization of the result: mahāmudrā. We aspire to become fortunate ones with that ability.

You may wonder whether anyone can maintain that unfabricated state right from the very beginning. Well, if one can, all the better. But since there are gradations in people's faculties, you may not have that ability. Then, as [Maitreyanātha] said,

> Through relying on reference points,
> the nonreferential itself will fully emerge.[35]

ཞེས་གསུངས་པ་ལྟར་སེམས་འཛིན་དམིགས་རྟེན་ཇི་ལྟར་རིགས་པ་
ལས་རིམ་པར་བསླབ་བོ། །

གཉིས་པ་རྒྱས་བཤད་ལ་གསུམ། ཞི་ལྷག་གི་ཆུལ་འཕྱོར། ཁམས་
རྣོགས་སྐྱེ་ཚུལ། བཅོ་སྟོང་ཟུང་འཇུག་གོ །དང་པོ་ལའང་གསུམ། ཞི་
གནས། ལྷག་མཐོང། ཟུང་འཇུག་གོ །དང་པོ་ཁ་ཞི་གནས་ཀ་ནི།

ཐུ་རགས་རྣོག་པའི་ཐ་ན་བྱབས་རང་ས་ཞི། །གཡོ་མེད་སེམས་ཀྱི་ཚུ
བོ་ངང་གིས་གནས། །ཕྱིང་ཆུགས་རྣོག་པའི་དྲི་མ་དང་བྲལ་བའི། །ཞི
གནས་རྒྱ་མཚོ་མི་གཡོ་བཏུན་པར་ཤོག

།ཅེས་གསུངས་ཏེ། མཇོད་ལས་དགྱོད་པ་དང་རྟོག་པ་ལ་ཐུ་རགས
སུ་བཤད་མོད་འདིར་མན་ངག་ཏུ། ཡུལ་ལ་འཇུག་པའི་རྟོག་དགྱོད
མཇོན་ཀྱར་མི་ཚོར་བའི་ཐུ་བ་དང། དེ་ཚོར་བའི་རགས་པ་སྟེ་སེམས
བྱང་རྟོག་པའི་དབའ་བླས་དེ་ཆེད་དུ་བཀག་པ་མ་ཡིན་པ་ངང
གིས་འགགས་པས་རང་ས་ཞི་གནས་གཡོ་ཏ་མེད་པར་སེམས་ཀྱི
ཚུ་བོ་དེ་ཉིད་ངང་གིས་གནས་ཤིང། ཕྱིང་ཆུགས་སོགས་བསམ་གཏན
གྱི་སྒྲིབ་པ་ལྷོང་རྟོག་པའི་དྲི་མ་ཐམས་ཅད་དང་བྲལ་བའི་ཞི་གནས
ཀྱི་རྒྱ་མཚོ་རྒྱུན་གང་གིས་ཀྱང་མི་གཡོ་བར་བཏུན་པ་མཐར་ཕྱིན
པར་ཤོག་ཅེག་ཅེས་པའོ། །བསམ་གཏན་གྱི་སྒྲིབ་པ་ལྟ་ནི། ཟུང་ཞབས
ཀྱི་བཤེས་སྒྲིངས་ལས་གསུངས་པ་ལྟར། ཡུལ་སྣ་ཚོགས་ལ་རྟོག་པ
འགྲོ་བའི་ཚོད་པ་དང། མི་རིགས་པ་བྱས་པ་ལ་འགྱོད་པ་གཉིས་ཀྱིས

In that way, train successively with whatever reference supports are suitable for gaining focused attention.

2) Extensive explanation

This has three parts: the yogas of calm abiding and higher insight, the way experience and realization arise, and the unity of love and emptiness.

a) Calm abiding and higher insight

i) Calm abiding

16. *The waves of subtle and coarse thoughts subside in themselves.*
The river of unmoved mind abides within itself.
Free of the murky stains of dullness and darkness,
may the unmoving ocean of calm abiding be steady.

Of course there are explanations of subtle and coarse discriminating concepts in the *Abhidharma*, but here we are concerned with the esoteric instructions. **Thoughts** and discriminations apprehending objective reality that are not evident or felt **are subtle** and those that are felt are **coarse**. Without blocking **the waves** of mental events and concepts on purpose, allow them to cease from within and **subside in themselves**. Then **the** broad **river of mind** will **abide without moving within** this **itself**, **free of** all **the stains** of drifting **murky** sediment. We aspire to reach the **ocean of calm abiding**, **steady and unmoved** by any conditions whatsoever, such as the **dullness and darkness** that obscure meditative **stability**.

སེམས་ཞི་བར་གནས་པའི་གེགས་བྱེད། གཙོ་དོ་སེམས་ཀྱིས་བདེ་བར་
གནས་པའི་གེགས་བྱེད། སེམས་འཕྲོས་པའི་བྱིང་བ་དང་དེ་བས་
ཆེར་བྱིང་བའི་རྒྱགས་པ་དང་གཏིད་དེ་གསུམ་ཀྱིས་གསལ་བར་
གནས་པའི་གེགས་བྱེད། ཡོ་བྱད་དང་སེམས་ཅན་ལ་ཆགས་པའི་
འདོད་འདུན་ཀྱིས་ལས་བྱང་དུ་གནས་པའི་གེགས་བྱེད། འདི་སྐོམ་
ཡིན་ནམ་མིན་སྙམ་པ་སོགས་ཐེ་ཚོམ་ཀྱིས་རྩེ་གཅིག་པར་གནས་
པའི་གེགས་བྱེད་པའོ། །ལྷ་པོ་དེའང་བསྟུ་ན། བྱིང་རྩོད་གཏིས་སུ་འདུ་
ལ་དེ་དག་སེལ་ཐབས་སོ་སོའི་གཏེན་པོ་བརྟེན་པ་དང། གཙོ་བོར་
བྱིང་རྩོད་ཀྱི་རང་ངོ་བལྟ་ཞིང་དེའི་ངོ་བོར་མ་བཅོས་པར་འཇོག་པ་
ཉིད་ཟབ་པར་གསུངས། ཕྱིར་ཉེས་པ་ལྟ་སྟོང་ཕྱིར་འདུ་བྱེད་བརྒྱད་
བརྟེན་པ་དང། སེམས་དགུ་ལ་མཉམ་བཞག་གྱུབ་ནས་བསམ་གཏན་
རྣམས་སྒྲུབ་པའི་ཚུལ་ཤེས་ནའང་ལེགས་སོ། །

གཏིས་པ་ལྟག་མཐོང་ལ་གཏིས། དངོས་དང། ཞི་རྩ་གཙོད་པའོ།
།དང་པོ་ཀ་ངོས་ཀ་ནི།

བལྟར་མེད་སེམས་ལ་ཡང་ཡང་བལྟས་པའི་ཚེ། །མཐོང་མེད་དོན་ནི་
ཇི་བཞིན་ལྟག་གིར་མཐོང། །ཡིན་མིན་དོན་ལ་ཐེ་ཚོམ་ཆོད་པ་ཉིད།
།འགྲུལ་མེད་རང་ངོ་རང་གིས་ཤེས་པར་ཤོག

The five obscurations of meditative stability according to Venerable Nāgārjuna in *Letter to a Friend*[36] are: (1) Agitation of the thoughts emanating to various objects and regret over inappropriate actions, both of which hinder the calm abiding of mind. (2) Malice hinders abiding in happiness. (3) Dullness of a heavy mind, and darkness that is even duller than that, and sleep; these three hinder abiding in clarity. (4) Desirous attachment to beings or things hinders effective abiding. (5) Doubts such as whether this is meditation or is not meditation hinder the abiding in undivided attention.

To condense those five, they can be included in two: dullness and agitation. You should rely on the antidotes of the specific methods to clear them up. The main thing is to look at the actual aspect of dullness and agitation and then settle in their essence without contrivance. This itself is said to be the most profound. In general, in order to eliminate these five flaws, it is also good to know the way to accomplish all meditative stability by relying on the eight remedies[37] and achieve equipoise by means of the nine methods of mental abiding.[38]

ii) Higher insight

This has two parts: the main part and severing the ground-root of peace.

(A) The main part, higher insight

17. *When you look again and again for imperceptible mind,*
you see distinctly the meaning of not seeing, just as it is.
Severing doubts about the meaning of being and nonbeing,
may I know my own unmistakable nature.

།ཅིས་གསུངས་ཏེ། བལྟ་བའི་ཡུལ་ལས་འདས་པས་བལྟ་བྱར་མེད་
པའི་སེམས་ཀྱི་གནས་ལུགས་དེ་ཉིད་ལ་མཉམ་པར་བཞག་ཅིང་བློ
མའི་མན་ངག་དང་སྨོན་བྱང་གི་ཤེས་རབ་ཀྱི་མིག་གིས་ཡང་དང
ཡང་དུ་བལྟས་པ་དེའི་ཚེ་མཐོང་བྱའི་དངོས་པོ་མེད་ཕྱིར་མཐོང་བ
དང་བྱལ་བའི་དོན་དེ་ཉིད་ནི་ཇི་ལྟ་བ་བཞིན་ལྟག་གེར་མཐོང་བས
ཡིན་མིན་ཡོད་མེད་སོགས་གནས་ལུགས་ཀྱི་དོན་དེ་ལ་སྒོ་སྐུར་དང
ཐེ་ཚོམ་ཚོད་པ་དེ་ཉིད་འགྲུལ་བ་མེད་པའི་རང་ངོ་རང་གིས་ཤེས
པའི་ཚུལ་དུ་ལྟག་མཐོང་གི་ཡེ་ཤེས་སྐྱེས་ནས་ལྟན་སྐྱེས་ཕྱག་རྒྱ་ཆེན
པོ་མངོན་དུ་འགྱུར་བར་མོག་ཅིག་ཅེས་པའོ། །དེའང་བསམ་པ་དང
སྨོན་པ་དང། ལྟ་བ་དང། ཤེས་པ་དང། མཐོང་བ་དང། ཐོང་བ་ལ
སོགས་པའི་མཚན་མ་ཐམས་ཅད་དང་བྲལ་བའི་གནས་ལུགས་ཤེས
པ་ལ་དེ་དང་དེར་བཏགས་པ་ཙམ་སྟེ། ཆད་སྟོང་མེད་དགག་ཙམ
ལ་ཡང་དག་པའི་དོན་དུ་བརྟུང་བ་བེམ་པོའི་སྟོང་ཉིད་དུ་བཤད་པ
སོགས་མ་རིག་པའི་ཕྱིན་གཡོག་དང་བྲལ་བས་རང་རིག་པ་དང། ཐུགས
འདོགས་དང་ཐེ་ཚོམ་ལ་སོགས་པ་ཚོད་པས་ངེས་པ་ཆེད་པ་དང། མི
བདེ་བའི་ཆས་པར་རྟོག་པའི་འགྱུར་བ་ཐམས་ཅད་སྤངས་པས་བདེ
བ་ཆེན་པོར་འཇོག་པ་སོགས་ཤེས་དགོས་པར་གསུངས་སོ། །

གཉིས་པ་གཞི་རྩ་གཅོད་པ་ནི།

ཡུལ་ལ་བལྟས་པས་ཡུལ་མེད་སེམས་སུ་མཐོང། །སེམས་ལ་བལྟས
པས་སེམས་མེད་ངོ་བོས་སྟོང། །གཉིས་ལ་བལྟས་པས་གཉིས་འཛིན
རང་ས་ར་ཐོལ།

Since the mind is beyond being a viewable object, rest in equipoise in the abiding nature of the very mind that is **not** something to **perceive. When you look again and again** with the eye of knowledge that comes from the guru's esoteric instructions and your own meditation, because no actual thing is there to be seen, at that time **you see distinctly** (*lhag ger mthong*; Skt. *vipaśyanā*) **the meaning** of the lack of **seeing** itself, **just as it is**. Through that insight, you **sever doubts** and superimpositions or denials **about the meaning of** the abiding nature, such as whether it is **being or nonbeing**, existent or nonexistent, and so forth. We aspire to develop the timeless awareness of higher insight and actualize innate mahāmudrā in that way of **unmistakably knowing one's own nature** oneself.

This knowledge of the abiding nature is free of all characteristics—such as contemplation, meditation, view, knowledge, insight, experience, and so forth—the mere designations of this or that. It is reflexive awareness because it is free of the veil of ignorance, such as the emptiness of dead matter explained in the nihilistic emptiness of mere negation that is mistaken as the genuine reality, and so forth. It is finding certitude, because it severs superimpositions and doubts. And it is the entrance into great happiness, since it eliminates all unhappy conceptual thoughts. You should know such things.

(B) Severing the underlying root

18. *When you look at objects, there are no objects, you see mind.*
Looking at mind, there is no mind; empty of essence.
Looking at both frees dualistic fixation in its own place.
May I realize lucid clarity, the abiding nature of mind.

།འོད་གསལ་སེམས་ཀྱི་གནས་ལུགས་རྟོགས་པར་མཛོག །ཅེས་གསུངས་
ཏེ། ཡུལ་རྒྱུ་གང་ཤར་གྱི་སྣང་བ་དེ་དག་གི་སྟེང་དུ་བལྟས་ནས་
མཉམ་པར་བཞག་པས་སྨོན་བྱང་གི་ཤེས་རབ་ཀྱིས་ཡུལ་ཆུམས་རང་
ངོ་མ་གྱུབ་པར་སེམས་ཙམ་དུ་མཐོང་ཞིང། དེ་བཞིན་དུ་སེམས་ཉིད་
ཀྱི་རང་ངོ་ལ་བལྟས་ནས་མཉམ་པར་བཞག་པས་སེམས་ཀྱང་གཞི་
མེད་ཙམ་བྱལ་ངོ་བོས་སྟོང་པར་རྟོགས་པ་དང། སྣང་སེམས་གཉིས་
རོ་མཉམ་དུ་མཉམ་པར་བཞག་ལ་བལྟས་པས་ཡུལ་ཡུལ་ཅན་ཀྱི་
གཉིས་འཛིན་གཞི་མེད་དུ་རང་སར་གྲོལ་ཏེ་རང་བཞིན་གྱིས་སྒྲིབ
པ་དང་བྲལ་བས་འོད་གསལ་བའི་སེམས་ཀྱི་གནས་ལུགས་ཇི་ལྟ་བ
བཞིན་རྟོགས་པར་མཛོག་ཅེས་པའོ། །འདི་སྐབས་ཁྱིད་རིམ་ཆུམས
ལ། སྣང་བ་སེམས། སེམས་སྟོང་པ། སྟོང་པ་ལྷུན་གྱུབ། ལྷུན་གྱུབ་རང
གྲོལ་དུ་ངོ་སྤྲོད་པར་གསུངས་ཏེ། གནས་ལུགས་ཐུགས་ཙམ་རྟོགས
ཀྱང་ཕྱིས་ནས་གཞི་ཙ་གཅོད་པའི་མན་ངག་གིས་ངོ་མ་སྦྱང་ན་ངེས
པ་ཆེད་དགོད་བར་གསུངས། དེའི་ཕྱིར་ངོ་འཕྲོད་ནས་ཀྱང་བློ་མའི
མན་ངག་གི་གནད་གསང་དང་ལྡན་པས་ཙལ་སྦྱངས་ཏེ་སྨོན་ལྟ
ཐོག་ཏུ་ཆྱེལ་དགོས་པར་མཉམ་མེད་བློ་མས་གསུངས་སོ། །དེ་ལྟར
ཡུལ་དང་སེམས་གཉིས་ཀ་ལ་ལྟ་བར་བྱེད་པ་ནི་ཤེས་རབ་གསུམ
ཀྱི་མིག་གིས་ཏེ། དེ་ལས་ཀྱང་ཆོས་ཉིད་ཇི་ལྟ་བ་བཞིན་མངོན་སུམ
དུ་མཐལ་བར་བྱེད་པ་ནི་སྨོན་བྱང་རྟོག་བྱལ་ཀྱི་ཤེས་རབ་ཉིད་ཡིན
པའི་ཕྱིར་བརྒྱུད་པ་འདིས་མཉམ་བཞག་ལ་དཔྱད་སྨོན་མི་མཛད་པ
ནི་གནད་གསང་བློ་ན་མེད་པར་བཞེད་དོ། །

When you look right **at** the appearances of whichever of the six sense **objects** arises, and then rest in equipoise, with the knowledge that comes from meditation **you** will **see** that there is only **mind**; **there are no objects** that exist from their own side. Likewise, when you **look** directly **at** the very essence of that **mind** itself and then rest in equipoise, you realize that **there is** also **no** underlying basis or root of **mind**; it is **empty of** an **essence**. Resting in the equipoise of the equal taste of **both** appearance and mind and **looking at** that, the **dualistic fixation** of object and subject is without basis, **free in its own place**. We aspire to realize just as it is **the lucid clarity of the abiding nature of mind**, which is naturally free of obscuration.

The guidance sequence for introducing mind's nature is taught as follows: appearances are introduced as mind, mind as empty, emptiness as spontaneously present, and spontaneous presence as naturally liberated. Even with a generalized realization of the abiding nature, it is said that later you will not gain certitude without the introduction through esoteric instructions of severing the underlying basic root. For that reason, the unequalled guru (Gampopa) said that you must train the energy with the secret vital points of the guru's instructions and convey that directly onto the meditation and view. The eyes of the three wisdoms can produce the view of both object and mind. However, only the nonconceptual wisdom that arises from meditation itself produces the actual encounter of the nature of phenomena or true reality. Therefore, in this lineage, analytic meditation is not done during meditative equipoise. This is considered the unsurpassable secret vital point.

གསུམ་པ་ཟུང་འཇུག་གི་རྣལ་འབྱོར་དེའི་མཚན་གྱི་རྣམ་གྲངས་ནི།

ཡིད་བྱེད་བཟལ་བ་འདི་ནི་ཕྱག་རྒྱ་ཆེ། །མཐའ་དང་བྲལ་བ་དབུ་མ་ཆེན་པོ་ཡིན། །འདི་ནི་ཀུན་འདུས་རྫོགས་ཆེན་ཞེས་བྱང་བྱ། །གཅིག་ཤེས་གྱིན་དོན་རྟོགས་པའི་གཏེང་འཕེལ་ཤོག

།ཅེས་གསུངས་ཏེ། ལྷན་སྐྱེས་ཡེ་ཤེས་ཏི་བཞིན་རྟོགས་ནས་མཉམ་པར་འཛོག་པའི་ཟུང་འཇུག་གི་རྣལ་འབྱོར་དེ་ནི་ཡིད་ལ་བྱེད་པ་ཐམས་ཅད་དང་བྲལ་བས་ན་འདི་ནི་ཕྱག་རྒྱ་ཆེན་པོ་ཞེས་བྱ་ལ། མཚན་གྱི་རྣམ་གྲངས་གཞན་ཡང། ཐོག་པའི་མཐའ་ཐམས་ཅད་དང་བྲལ་བས་ན་དབུ་མ་ཆེན་པོའང་འདི་ཉིད་ཡིན་ལ། འདིར་ནི་ཆོས་ཀུན་གྱི་རྟོགས་པ་འདུས་པའི་ཕྱིར་རྫོགས་པ་ཆེན་པོ་ཞེས་བྱང་བྱ་སྟེ་དེ་བཞིན་ཉིད་གཅིག་པུ་འདི་ཁོ་ན་ཤེས་པས་ཆོས་རྣམས་ཀུན་གྱི་དོན་གྱི་གནད་གསང་མ་ལུས་པ་རྟོགས་པས་གཏེང་འཕེལ་པར་ཤོག་ཅེས་པའོ། །ཀུང་གི་སྒྲས་ཟབ་པ་དང་རྒྱ་ཆེ་བའི་ཆོས་ཐམས་ཅད་ཀྱི་དོན་དང་མཚན་ཐམས་ཅད་འདིར་འདུས་པར་སྟོན་ཅིང་རྒྱ་མཚན་དེས་གཅིག་ཤེས་ཀུན་གསོལ་བ་བསྟུབ་པར་མཛད་པའང་ཡིན་ཏེ། འདི་ལ་དགོངས་ནས་བདེ་གཤེགས་ཕགས་མོ་ཀུ་པས། རྣམ་རྟོག་དང་ནི་ཉོན་མོངས་པ། ।ཐམས་ཅད་འདུལ་བས་འདུལ་བ་ཡིན། ।རྣམ་པར་རྟོག་པ་ཆོས་སྐུ་བུ། ।ངེས་པའི་ཤེས་པ་སྐྱེད་པའི་ས། ।གྲོལ་འདོགས་ནང་ནས་གཅོད་པས་ན། ।འདི་ནི་བླ་མའི་གདམས་ངག་ཡིན། ।འཕོར་དང་ཆུང་ངན་འདས་པའི་ཆོས། ।ཞེམས་ནུ་རྫོགས་པས་རྫོགས་ཆེན་ཡིན། ।བཟང་རྟོག་ངན་རྟོག་ཐམས་ཅད་ཀུན། ।ཡིད་ལ་

iii) The yoga of unity: the synonyms

19. *Free of mental engagement; this is mahāmudrā.*
Free of extremes; this is mahāmadhyamaka.
All-inclusive, it is also called mahāsandhi.
May I gain confidence that knowing one is realizing all.

Once you have realized innate timeless awareness just as it is, the unified yoga of resting in that equipoise is **free of all mental engagement. This is** called **mahāmudrā** ("great seal"). Other synonyms are enumerated. Because it is **free of all extremes** of embellishment, the **mahāmadhyamaka** ("great middle way") **is** also **this** very thing. In this is **included** the realization of **all** phenomena, so **it is also called mahāsandhi** ("great completion"). Through **knowing this one** thing, we aspire to **gain** the **confidence** of **realizing all** the secret vital points of the meaning of **all** phenomena.

The word "also" indicates that all characteristics and meanings of the vast and profound Dharma are included in this. Therefore this also establishes that "knowing one liberates all." Having pondered this, Sugata Pakmo Drupa stated:

All concepts and afflictions are tamed,
so this is the Vinaya.
It is the source of the certain knowledge
that all conceptual thoughts are dharmakāya.
As all embellishment is severed from within,
this is the instruction of the guru.
[Eternalism, nihilism, impositions, denials;
free of all such extremes, it is the middle way.
Being unutterable, unthinkable, and inexpressible,

མི་བྱེད་ཕྱག་རྒྱ་ཆེ། །ལྷག་བསྟལ་ཞི་བས་ཞི་བྱེད་ཡིན། །ཁོན་མོངས་
དང་ནི་ཆུམ་རྐོག་ཀུན། །ལམ་དུ་སློང་བས་གསང་སྦྱགས་ཡིན།
།ས་མས་དང་ཆུམ་རྐོག་ཆོས་སྐུ་གསུམ། །དང་པོ་ལྷན་ཅིག་སྐྱེས་པ་སྟེ།
།གདན་ས་པས་གཅིག་ཏུ་སྤྱོར་བའི་ཕྱིར། །ལྷན་ཅིག་སྐྱེས་སྤྱོར་ཞེས་
སུ་བཤད། །འདི་དང་བདུད་ལ་སོགས་པ་ཡི། །བར་གཅོད་ལ་ཡང་
བསྟན་པ་གསུངས། །ཞེས་དང། ཨ་རྡ་གས་བྱམ་སྒྲབ་ཞལ་གདན་ས་
ལས་གསུངས་པ་ལྟ་བུས་མཚོན་ནོ། །

གཉིས་པ་ཉམས་རྐོགས་སྐྱེ་ཚུལ་ལ། ཉམས་དང། རྐོགས་པ་གཉིས་
ལས། དང་པོ་ཉམས་སྐྱེ་ཚུལ་ཞེ་ནི།

ཞེན་པ་མེད་པའི་བདེ་ཆེན་རྒྱུན་ཆད་མེད། །མཚན་འཛིན་མེད་པའི
འོད་གསལ་སྒྲིབ་གཡོག་བྲལ། །བློ་ལས་འདས་པའི་མི་རྟོག་ལྷུན་གྱིས
གྲུབ། །རྩོལ་མེད་ཉམས་ཐོབ་རྒྱུན་ཆད་མེད་པར་ཤོག

།ཅེས་གསུངས་ཏེ། དེ་ལྟར་ཞི་ལྷག་གི་རྣལ་འབྱོར་ལ་མཉམ་པར
བཞག་པས་སྐྱོན་དང་བྲལ་བའི་ཉམས་གསུམ་སྐྱེ་སྟེ། ཞེན་པ་མེད

it is the instruction on the Perfection of Wisdom.]
Since all phenomena of samsara and nirvana
are complete within mind, it is the great completion.
Not engaging good thoughts and bad thoughts
in the mind, it is the great seal.
It is pacification[39] since it pacifies suffering.
Since all afflictions and conceptual thoughts
are taken as the path, it is secret mantra.
Mind, thoughts, and dharmakāya—
these three are innate from the start.
Since they are applied as one by instructions,
they are taught as applied coemergence.
It is even acclaimed as the severance[40]
of obstructing demons, devils, and so on.[41]

This is also indicated by such teachings as the direct instructions for the vase consecration by Arāga.[42]

b) How experience and realization arise

i) How experience arises

20. *The great bliss free of attachment is continuous.*
Lucid clarity without fixation on attributes is free of obscuring veils.
Nonthought beyond intellect is spontaneously present.
May these experiences occur continuously without effort.

Three flawless experiences arise from resting in the equipoise of the yogas of calm abiding and higher insight: the experience of **continuous great bliss free of attachment**; the experience of

པའི་བདེ་བ་ཆེན་པོ་རྒྱུན་ཆད་མེད་པའི་ཉམས་དང། ཡུལ་ལ་མཚན་
མར་འཛིན་པ་མེད་པའི་རང་རིག་བོད་གསལ་སྒྲིབ་གཡོགས་བྲལ་
བའི་ཉམས་དང། བློའི་སྟོང་ཡུལ་ལས་འདས་པའི་མི་རྟོག་པ་སྟོང་པ་
ཉིད་ལྷུན་གྱིས་གྲུབ་པའི་ཉམས་ཏེ་བདེ་གསལ་མི་རྟོག་པའི་ཉམས་
གསུམ་གཉིས་འཕྲད་དུ་རེ་བ་དང་མ་ཐུང་གིས་དོགས་པ་སོགས་
ཀྱིས་མི་བསླད་པར་གཉུག་མའི་ངང་དུ་ལ་བཟློས་ཀྱང་རྩོལ་མེད་
རང་ཤུགས་ཀྱིས་ཉམས་སྐྱོང་རྒྱུན་ཆད་མེད་པ་འཕྲད་བར་ཤོག་ཅིག
ཅེས་པའོ། །དེ་ལས་ལྷོག་པ་ནི་སྐྱོན་ཅན་གོལ་ས་ཡིན་པས་རེ་དོགས་
འཛིན་ཞེན་མེད་པར་གཉུག་མའི་ངང་དུ་རོ་མཉམ་པས་ཟུང་འཇུག
གི་ཚུལ་ཟློགས་ཏེ་དེས་ཡོན་ཏན་ཐམས་ཅད་འཕྲད་ལ། དཔལ་ས
ར་ཏཱ། ཞེམས་འགགས་པ་དང་ཆུང་འགགས་པ། ། དཔལ་ལྷན་ཕ
མའི་མན་ངག་ཡིན། །ཞེས་གསུངས་པ་ལྟར་ཞེམས་ཟིན་པས་ཆུང
ཟིན། དེས་དོས་སྐྱེ། དེས་བདེ་བ་སྐྱེ། དེ་ལ་བརྟེན་ནས་གསལ་བ་དང
མི་རྟོག་པཤད་འཕྲད་པས་གནད་འདིས་ཁྱིད་སྲོལ་འདི་ལ་ཐབས
ལམ་སོགས་ཆེད་དུ་མ་བསྟོམས་ཀྱང་རྒྱས་བཅུ་ལ་སོགས་པ་སྒྲགས
ལམ་གྱི་དོད་རྒྱས་ནམས་ཇི་ལྟ་བ་བཞིན་འཕྲད་པ་སོགས་རྒྱ་ཆེར
གསུངས་པ་ཡོད་དོ། །

གཉིས་པ་རྟོགས་པ་སྐྱེ་ཚུལ་ནི།

བཟང་ཞེན་ཉམས་ཀྱི་འཛིན་པ་རང་ས་ར་གྲོལ། ।ངན་རྟོག་འགྲུལ་པ
ར་ང་བཞིན་དབྱིངས་སུ་དག ।ཐ་མལ་ཤེས་པ་སྒང་བློ་བྲལ་ཐོབ
མེད། ।སྒོམ་བྲལ་ཆོས་ཉིད་བདེན་པ་རྟོགས་པར་ཤོག

lucid clarity free of obscuring veils, which is reflexive awareness **without fixation on** the **attributes** of objects; and the experience of **nonthought beyond** the sphere of **intellect**, **spontaneously present** emptiness. Reaching resolution within the innate state free of contamination, such as hopes for their arising or fears that they won't arise, we aspire that **these** felt **experiences occur continuously** on their own strength **without effort**.

Since the opposites of those are flawed deviations, cultivate equal taste within the innate state without hopes and fears, fixation, and clinging. That is the consummate expression of unity through which all good qualities will arise. Glorious Saraha said,

> Stilling the mind and stilling the winds
> is the glorious guru's esoteric instruction.[43]

As that suggests, controlling the mind causes control of the vital winds. That produces heat, which produces bliss. Based on that, clarity and nonthought will also occur. Through this vital point, even if you do not intentionally meditate on the path of methods in this guidance system, the signs of warmth in the Mantra Vehicle, such as the ten signs,[44] will arise just as they should. This and other subjects are taught extensively.

ii) How realization arises

21. *Attachment fixated on good experience subsides on its own.*
Delusion of bad thought is naturally pure in basic space.
Ordinary mind is free of acceptance and rejection, loss and gain.
May I realize the truth of unembellished true reality.

།ཅིས་གསུངས་ཏེ། བཤད་མ་ཐག་པའི་ཁམས་ལ་བཟང་རྟོག་ཞེན་
འཛིན་སོགས་ཁམས་ཀྱི་འཛིན་པ་མཐའ་དག་རང་སར་ཡོལ་ཞིང།
ཆོས་གཡེང་གི་རྩེས་སུ་འཕྲེང་བའི་ངན་རྟོག་འཕྲལ་པ་ཐམས་ཅད་
ཀྱང་ཆེད་དུ་མ་སྦངས་ཀྱང་མཁམ་བཞག་གི་མཐུས་རང་བཞིན་གྱིས་
དེ་ཁོ་ན་ཉིད་ཀྱི་དབྱིངས་སུ་དག་པས་ཐ་མལ་གྱི་ཤེས་པ་ཞེས་གཏུག
མའི་སེམས་དེ་ཉིད་མངོན་དུ་གྱུར་ཏེ། སྦང་བྱ་སྒྲིབ་པའི་ཚོས་གང
ཡང་སྦངས་པ་མེད་པའི་ཚུལ་ཁོང་དུ་ཆུད་པ་དང། དེ་བཞིན་དུ་བླང
བྱ་གཉིས་པོའི་ཚོས་དང་སྦངས་པ་ལས་བྱུང་བའི་བྱལ་བ་དང་སྦངས
བླངས་བྱས་པས་ཐོབ་པའི་འཕྲས་བུ་དང་བཅས་པ་དེ་དང་དེའི
རང་བཞིན་དུ་མེད་ཅིང་མི་གནས་པའི་ཚུལ་ཇི་ལྟ་བ་བཞིན་ཁོང་དུ
ཆུད་པས་སྐྱེ་འགག་རྒྱ་ཆད་འགྲོ་འོང་གཅིག་ཐ་དད་སོགས་སྟོས
པའི་མཐའ་ཐམས་ཅད་དང་བྲལ་བའི་ཚོས་ཉིད་ཀྱི་བདེན་པ་རྟོགས
པར་ཕོག་ཅིག་ཅེས་པའོ། །འགོར་འདས་བདེན་གཉིས་སོགས་གང
ཡང་མི་དམིགས་པའི་གཉིས་མེད་ནི་ཚོས་ཉིད་ཀྱི་བདེན་པ་ཡིན་ལ
དེ་རྟོགས་ན་བླང་དོར་སོགས་ཀྱི་མཚན་མ་སྟོག་རང་བཙལ་དུ་འགྲོ
ཞིང་དེ་མིན་བླང་དོར་ཀྱི་མཚན་མ་རང་ཞིར་འགྱུར་མི་སྲིད་པ་ཀུན
མཁྱེན་རྩེས་གསུངས་སོ། །

གསུམ་པ་བཅུ་སྟོང་ཟུང་འཇུག་གི་ཁམས་ལེན་ལ་སྟོན་པ་ལ་གཉིས།
ཐོག་རྩེ་ངོས་བཟུང་བ། དེ་སྟོང་ཉིད་དང་ཟུང་དུ་འཇུག་ཚུལ་བོ།
།དང་པོ་ཁ་ཐོག་རྩེ་ངོས་བཟུང་བ་ཀ། ནི།

Regarding those experiences just described, all **fixation on experience**, such as that it is **good**, or conceit, **attachment**, fixation and so on, **subside in their own** place. All the **delusional bad thoughts** that follow after total distraction [from meditation], even without being deliberately rejected, will be **naturally pure** in the **basic space** of suchness on the strength of your meditative equipoise. So-called **ordinary mind**, the innate mind itself, fully manifests. You should master the way of nonrejection of obscuring phenomena that are [normally] objects of **rejection**. Similarly, with what [is normally] **accepted**—the remedial teachings of antidotes, the **loss** produced by rejection, and the resulting **gains** from rejection and acceptance—master precisely how that and its intrinsic nature are nonexistent and nonabiding. We aspire to **realize the truth** of **reality**, which is **free of** all extremes of **embellishment**, such as birth, cessation, permanence, extinction, going, coming, single, or many.

Nonduality is without any reference points, such as samsara and nirvana, the two truths, and so forth. This is the truth of reality. When that is realized, the ties to attributes, such as what to adopt and discard, are released. Barring that, it is not possible for the characteristics of adopting and discarding to resolve themselves, according to the omniscient lord.

c) The unity of love and emptiness

The aspiration to practice the unity of love and emptiness has two parts: identifying compassion and how that is unified with emptiness.

i) Identifying compassion

འགྲོ་བའི་རང་བཞིན་རྣག་ཏུ་སངས་རྒྱས་ཀྱང། །མ་རྟོགས་དབང་
གིས་མཐའ་མེད་འཁོར་བར་འཁྱམས། །སྡུག་བསྔལ་མུ་མཐའ་མེད་
པའི་ཕེམས་ཅན་ལ། །བཟོད་མེད་སྙིང་རྗེ་རྒྱུད་ལ་སྐྱེ་བར་ཤོག

།ཅེས་གསུངས་ཏེ། འགྲོ་བ་མ་ལུས་པའི་རང་བཞིན་ནི་དུས་རྣག་ཏུ་
སངས་རྒྱས་ཆོས་སྐུའི་ངོ་བོ་ཡིན་འདུག་ཀྱང་དེ་ལྟར་མ་རྟོགས་པའི་
དབང་གིས་མཐའ་མེད་པའི་འཁོར་བར་འཁྱམས་ཤིང་སྡུག་བསྔལ་
རྣམ་པ་སྟོ་ཚོགས་མུ་མཐའ་མེད་པར་མྱོང་བའི་ཕ་མར་ཀྱུར་པའི་
ཕེམས་ཅན་ཐམས་ཅད་ལ་བཟོད་གླགས་མེད་པའི་སྙིང་རྗེ་དྲག་པོ་
རྒྱུན་མི་འཆད་པ་རྒྱུད་ལ་སྐྱེ་བར་ཤོག་ཅེག་ཅེས་པའོ། །ཕྱི་མ་དམ་
པའི་མན་ངག་ཚུལ་བཞིན་ཉམས་སུ་བླངས་པས་གནས་ལུགས་
ཀྱི་དོན་གཤའ་མ་རྟོགས་ཚོ་དེ་ལྟར་སྐྱེ་བའང་ཆོས་ཉིད་ཡིན་པར་
གསུངས་ཏེ། མདོ་ལས། བྱང་ཆུབ་ཕེམས་དཔའ་མཉམ་བཞག་པས།
།གོམས་པའི་སྟོབས་ཀྱིས་རྫོགས་པ་ནི། ।དངོས་འཛིན་གདོན་ཀྱིས་
ཟིན་པ་ལ། ।ཁྱད་པར་དུ་ཡང་སྙིང་རྗེ་སྐྱེ། ।ཞེས་དང།

འཕགས་པ་གྲུ་སྒྲོག་ཀྱིས། དེ་ལྟར་སྟོང་པ་ཉིད་འདི་ནི། ।རྣལ་འབྱོར་
པ་ཡིས་བསྒོམས་བྱས་ན། । གཞན་ཀྱི་དོན་ལ་ཆགས་པའི་བློ། ।འཁྱུང
བར་འགྱུར་བ་ཐེ་ཚོམ་མེད། ।ཅེས་དང། མཉམ་མེད་དཔགས་པོས།

22. Though the nature of migrators is ever buddha,
they fail to realize it and wander endlessly in samsara.
May unbearable compassion be born in my being
for endlessly suffering sentient beings.

The nature of all **migrators** without exception has **forever** been that of a **buddha**, present as the essence of dharmakāya. **Though** this is so, **they fail to realize it** as such and **wander endlessly in samsara**, experiencing an **endless** variety of **suffering**. We aspire that intense, unrelenting **compassion** that is **not possible to bear is born in our being for** all those **sentient beings** that have been our mothers and fathers.

At such time as the true meaning of the abiding nature arises through properly taking into practice the esoteric instructions of the holy guru, that is taught to be the true reality. It states in a sutra:

> The bodhisattva who has mastered equipoise
> on the strength of familiarization
> develops compassion particularly for those
> in the grip of the spirit of belief in reality.[45]

And Noble Nāgārjuna said,

> When a yogin thus meditates
> on this emptiness,
> an attitude of caring for others' welfare
> will no doubt arise.[46]

Incomparable Dakpo said,

དོན་དམ་རྟོགས་ན་བྱམས་སྙིང་རྗེ་གཞན་དོན་དུ་འཕྲུང་བ་རྒྱུ་འབྲས་ཡིན། ཁོན་མོངས་ཤུགས་ཀྱིས་ལྷོག་པ་ཡིན། ངོ་བོ་རྟོགས་ཟེར་ཡང་མི་དགེ་བ་ལ་འཇུག ཏྲམས་སྙིང་རྗེ་བྱང་ཆུབ་ཀྱི་ས་ཞིམས་ཆུང་བར་འདུག་ན་ངོ་བོ་མ་རྒྱུས་པ་ཡིན། ཏླ་མ་རྗེ་བཅུན་གྱིས་གསུངས་པ་དེ་ཡིན་གསུངས།

དེས་ན་སྟོང་ཉིད་རྟོགས་པས་བདག་ལ་གཅིས་འཛིན་བྱལ་ཞིང་དེ་ལྟར་མ་རྟོགས་པའི་འགྲོ་ལ་སྙིང་རྗེའི་དབང་གིས་སྲིད་ལས་གྲོལ་ཡང་སྲིད་པ་བཟུང་ནས་འགོར་བ་ཇི་སྲིད་དུ་སྲིད་པར་གནས་ཀྱང་དེའི་སྨོན་ཀྱིས་མ་གོས་པར་ཆུའི་པདྨ་བཞིན་འགྲོ་དོན་མཛད་པ་ནི་རྒྱལ་སྲས་འཕགས་པ་ཞེས་བྱ་སྟེ། ཟུ་ཞབས་ཀྱིས།

བསམ་གཏན་བདེ་བ་གོར་ནས་ཀྱང། །མནར་མེད་པར་ཡང་འཇུག་པར་བྱེད། །འདི་ནི་ངོ་མཚར་འདི་བསྟན་འོས། །ཞེས་སོགས་རྒྱ་ཆེར་གསུངས་པ་ལྟར་རོ། །

གཉིས་པ་ཏི་ཀྵ་ཉིད་དང་ཟུང་དུ་འཇུག་ཚུལ་ཝ་ནི།

བཟོད་མེད་སྙིང་རྗེའི་ཚལ་ཡང་མ་འགགས་པའི། །བཅོ་དྲུག་ངོ་བོ་སྟོང་དོན་རྗེན་པར་ཤར། །ཟུང་འཇུག་གོལ་ས་བྱལ་བའི་ལམ་མཆོག་འདི། །འཕྲལ་མེད་ཉིད་མཚན་ཀུན་ཏུ་བསྐོམ་པར་ཤོག

།ཅེས་གསུངས་ཏེ། དེ་ལྟར་བཟོད་གླགས་མེད་པའི་སྙིང་རྗེ་ཆེན་པོའི་

> When you realize the absolute, love and compassion and altruism develop—this is cause and effect. The opposite is true for the power of afflictions. To say you realize the essence but engage in nonvirtue with little love, compassion, and awakening mind [means that realization of] the essence has in fact not arisen. So said my guru Jetsun [Milarepa].[47]

Therefore, the realization of emptiness is free of self-cherishing. Through the power of compassion for those who do not have that realization, though you could be liberated from existence, you hold on to existence and remain for as long as existence exists. But like a lotus in water, you are not sullied by its flaws. Someone who enacts the welfare of migrators in this way is known as an Exalted Child of the Victor. This is taught widely, such as this by Nāgārjuna:

> Abandoning the bliss of concentration,
> they would even enter Incessant Hell.
> This is amazing and worthy of praise.[48]

ii) How compassion is unified with emptiness

23. *Unimpeded energy of unbearable compassion is love,*
the meaning of its empty essence exposed.
This supreme path of unity that never deviates;
may I meditate on this day and night without interruption.

The energy of such great **unbearable compassion** also arises **unimpededly** and within that state **is love**. At that

རྒྱལ་དེ་ཡང་མ་འགགས་པར་འཚར་བཞིན་པའི་ངང་བཅུ་དུས་དེ་
ཉིད་ན་གནས་ལུགས་གཉིས་མེད་ཡེ་ཤེས་ངོ་བོ་སྟོང་པ་ཉིད་ཀྱི་དོན་
ཡང་མངོན་སུམ་རྟེན་པར་ཤར་བས་སྟོང་ཉིད་སྙིང་རྗེ་རོ་མཉམ་དུ་
འདྲེས་པའི་ཟུང་འཇུག་ནི་སྲིད་ཞིའི་གོལ་ས་བྲལ་བའི་ལམ་མཆོག
མི་གནས་པའི་མྱང་འདས་བློ་མེད་ཟློག་ཏུང་འཛིན་པའི་རྒྱ་དངོས
ཡིན་པས་འདི་ཉིད་རྒྱ་རྟེ་ཚེ་འཚང་གི་གོ་འཕང་ནམ་ཐོབ་ཀྱི་བར་དུ
རྒྱུན་གྱིས་འབྱལ་བ་མེད་པར་ཉིན་མཚན་ཀུན་ཏུ་བསྒོམ་པར་ཤོག
ཅེག་ཅེས་པའོ།།

གསུམ་པ་སྟོང་པས་མཐར་དབྱུང་བ་ནི། ཕྱགས་ལས་བསྟན་ཏེ། དེ
ལྟར་སྒོམ་པས་ཉམས་སུ་ལེན་པའི་ཚུལ་བསྟན་པ་ཉིད་གོམས་པ
བློང་དུ་འགྱུར་བའི་ཕྱིར་མོས་གུས་སྒོམ་གྱི་མགོ་བོ་ལ་སྙིང་ལུར
བཞུগས་ཏེ་གཞི་བཅས། ཞེན་ཡོག་སྒོམ་གྱི་ཆུང་པས་ཚེ་འདིའི་འདོད
འདུན་འཇིག་རྟེན་ཚེས་བཏུང་གྱི་གདོས་ཐག་བཅད། ཡེངས་མེད
སྒོམ་གྱི་དངོས་གཞི་སྒྲུབ་ཚུགས་རི་ལྟར་དུ་བརྟན་པས་སྒོམ་མེད
ཀྱི་རྒྱལ་སར་སྐྱེག་པ་ནི་སྟོས་མེད་ཐུ་སུ་ཀུའི་སྟོད་པ་ཞེས་སྟོད་པ
ཆུམས་ཀྱི་ནང་ནས་མཚོག་ཏུ་ཐུར་པ་བཀའ་བཏུད་གྱབ་ཐོབ་རྒྱ་མཚོ
གཤེགས་པའི་བཤུལ་ལམ་ཆད་དུ་ཐུང་བ་སྟེ། གོང་དུ་སྒོམ་དོན་ཀུན
ལ་རྒྱལ་སྟོང་སྟོང་པའི་མཚོག་གསུངས་པ་ཉིད་དོ།།

ལྔ་པ་ལམ་མཐར་ཕྱིན་པའི་འབྲས་བུ་ལ་སྨོན་པ་ནི།

བསྒོམས་སྟོབས་ལས་བྱུང་སྦྱན་དང་མངོན་ཤེས་དང། ཁེམས་ཅན

very moment, the timeless awareness of the nondual abiding nature, **the meaning of essential emptiness**, also manifests and is **exposed**. The **unity** of emptiness and compassion blended as a single taste is the **supreme path that never deviates** into existence or peace. This is the actual cause for attaining nonabiding nirvana or unsurpassable perfect awakening. Therefore, until the time of attaining the state of Vajradhara, we aspire to **meditate on this** constantly, **day and night without interruption** by circumstances.

C) Reaching the ultimate through conduct

This is presented implicitly because one attains full mastery through familiarizing oneself with this very teaching on how to practice meditation in this manner. "Devotion, the head of meditation," means that an unwavering heart is the foundation. "Revulsion, the foot of meditation," is to decisively cut off the yearning desires of this life and the eight worldly concerns. "Nondestraction, the body of meditation," is to firmly establish practice like a mountain. Therefore, to reach the domain of nonmeditation, the so-called unembellished *bhusuku* conduct[49] is the most excellent of all the conducts. It is the path traveled by the ocean of Kagyü adepts, left as an amazing legacy. The energy training in all the meditation topics described above are themselves the supreme conduct. So it is said.

5. Aspiration for the ultimate result of the path

24. *With the eyes and clairvoyances produced by potent meditation,*

སྒོམ་བྱས་སངས་རྒྱས་ཞིང་རབ་སྦྱངས། །སངས་རྒྱས་ཆོས་རྣམས་འགྲུབ་པའི་སྒོམ་ལམ་རྫོགས། །རྫོགས་སྒོམ་སྦྱངས་གསུམ་མཐར་ཕྱིན་སངས་རྒྱས་ཤོག

།ཅེས་གསུངས་ཏེ། དེ་ལྟར་མོས་གུས་བླ་མའི་བྱིན་རླབས་ཀྱི་ཤེར་ལམ་ལ་བརྟེན་པའི་ཕྱག་རྒྱ་ཆེན་པོའི་གདམས་ངག་ཕྱིན་ཅི་མ་ལོག་པ་བསྐོམས་པའི་སྟོབས་ཀྱིས་བྱང་བའི་འཕགས་བུ་སྦྱན་ལྟ་དང། མངོན་པར་ཤེས་པ་རྡུག་རྣམས་ཡོངས་སུ་དག་པའི་ཡོན་ཏན་དང་ལྡན་པས་སེམས་ཅན་ཐམས་ཅད་སྒྲོལ་བར་བྱས་ཤིང། སངས་རྒྱས་ཀྱི་ཞིང་རབ་འབྱམས་མཐའ་ཡས་པ་སྦྱངས་ནས། སངས་རྒྱས་ཀྱི་ཆོས་གཞན་དང་ཐུན་མོང་མ་ཡིན་པའི་སྐུ་དང་ཡེ་ཤེས་ཡོན་ཏན་ཕྲིན་ལས་རྣམས་ཡོངས་སུ་གྲུབ་པའི་སྒོམ་ལམ་འབྱམ་ཐུག་བཅུ་འཁོར་དང་བཅས་པ་མཐའ་དག་རྫོགས་པ་དང། དེ་ལྟར་རྫོགས་སྒྲོལ་སྦྱངས་གསུམ་ཐམས་ཅད་མཐར་ཕྱིན་ནས་བླ་ན་མེད་པ་རྫོགས་པའི་སངས་རྒྱས་ཀྱི་གོ་འཕང་མྱུར་དུ་ཐོབ་པར་གོག་ཅིག་ཅེས་པའོ། །དེའང་ལམ་དུས་སུ་ཐོག་མར་མངོན་ཤེས་སོགས་བསྒྲིད་ནས་རིམ་གྱིས་རྫོགས་སྒྲོལ་སྦྱངས་གསུམ་མཐར་དབྱུང་དགོས་པས་ན་འདིར་ཡང་ཐོག་མར་སྦྱན་དང་མངོན་ཤེས་ཉིད་གསུངས་པ་སྟེ། དེ་ལ་སྦྱན་ལྟ་ནི། མདོ་ལས། བྱང་ཆུབ་སེམས་དཔའི་ཤའི་མིག་གིས་དཔག་ཚད་བཀྲ་ནས་སྟོང་གསུམ་གྱི་སྟོང་ཆེན་པོའི་འཇིག་བརྟེན་གྱི་ཁམས་མཐོང་བར་གསུངས་པ་ནི་ཤའི་སྦྱན་དང། རྒྱལ་ཆེན་བཞི་རིས་པ་རྣམས་ནས་བོག་མིན་བར་གྱི་ལྟ་རྣམས་ཀྱི་ལྟའི་མིག་དེ་ནི་བྱང་ཆུབ་སེམས་

sentient beings are matured and buddha fields refined.
Aspirations for accomplishing buddha qualities are fulfilled.
May I become buddha, the ultimate fulfillment, maturation,
and refinement.

The five **eyes and** the six **clairvoyances** are the result **produced by** the **potent meditation** on unerring instructions of mahāmudrā based on the fast path of devotion and the blessings of the guru. **With** these completely pure qualities, all **sentient beings are matured and** the infinite **buddha realms** without limit are **refined**. A million **aspirations** and their offshoots **for accomplishing** other **buddha qualities** and extraordinary bodies, awarenesses, qualities, and activities are totally **fulfilled**. In this way, after reaching the **ultimate** stage of these three—**fulfillment, maturation, and refinement**—we aspire to quickly attain the state of unsurpassed perfect **buddha**.

At the time of the path, first the clairvoyances and so on are produced and then gradually the fulfillment, maturation, and refinement must be brought to consummation. Therefore, here the eyes and clairvoyances were taught first.

The five eyes [or sights] are taught in the sutras:

(1) With the physical eyes the bodhisattvas can see from one hundred leagues up to all the billion world realms in the universe. (2) The divine eye is possessed by all the gods from the realms of the four great kings up to the unsurpassed realm Akaniṣṭha. It is said that bodhisattvas fully comprehend that sight, but the gods do not comprehend the divine eye that bodhisattvas possess. That is because over and above that

དཔལ་རབ་ཏུ་ཤེས་ལ་བྱང་ཆུབ་སེམས་དཔའི་ལྷའི་མིག་དེ་ནི་ལྷ་
དེ་ཆུམས་ཀྱིས་མི་ཤེས་པར་གསུངས་པས་ལྷའི་མིག་དེ་ལས་ཁྱད་
པར་འཕགས་པ་ཐོགས་བཅུའི་སེམས་ཅན་ཐམས་ཅད་ཀྱི་འཚེ་འགོ་
དང་རྒྱུ་བ་གཟིགས་པ་ལྷའི་སྤྱན་དང། བདག་མེད་ཇི་བཞིན་རྟོགས་
པའི་ཤེས་རབ་ནི་ཤེས་རབ་ཀྱི་སྤྱན་དང། སྟོབ་དཔོན་དབྱིག་གཉེན་
གྱིས་བཞེད་པ་ལྟར་གནས་དང་གནས་མིན་མཁྱེན་པའི་སྟོབས་མ་
གཏོགས་སྟོབས་དགུ་པོ་ཆུམས་ནི་ཆོས་ཀྱི་སྤྱན་དང། ཆོས་ཐམས་ཅད་
ཆུམ་པ་ཐམས་ཅད་དུ་མངོན་པར་རྫོགས་པ་རྟོགས་པ་ནི་སངས་
རྒྱས་ཀྱི་སྤྱན་ཏེ་ལྷའོ། །མངོན་ཤེས་དྲུག་ནི། རྫུ་འཕྲུལ་ཀྱི་ཆོ་འཕྲུལ་
མཐའ་ཡས་པར་སྟོན་པའི་རྫུ་འཕྲུལ་མངོན་པར་ཤེས་པ། མཐའ་ཡས་
པའི་ཞིང་གི་སྒྲ་ཐོས་པའི་ལྷའི་ཆ་བ་མངོན་པར་ཤེས་པ་སེམས་ཅན་
ཐམས་ཅད་ཀྱི་སེམས་ཀྱི་ཚུལ་ཇི་ལྟ་བར་སོ་སོར་ཤེས་པའི་གཞན་
སེམས་མངོན་པར་ཤེས་པ། སེམས་ཅན་ཆུམས་ཀྱི་སྐྱེ་འཚེ་ལས་དང་
འབྲས་བུའི་ཚུལ་དང་བཅས་ཤེས་པའི་ལྷའི་མིག་མངོན་པར་ཤེས་པ།
གྲྭོ་ཐོགས་མཐའ་དག་ཏོ་བོ་ཉིད་ཀྱི་མི་གནས་པས་རབ་ཏུ་སྦྱངས་
པའི་ཟག་པ་ཟད་པ་མངོན་པར་ཤེས་པ་དང་དྲུག་གོ། ལྷའི་མིག་ལ
ས་ཆུམ་སྨིན་ལས་སྐྱེས་པ་དང། ཕྱི་མ་བསྒོམས་སྟོབས་ལས་སྐྱེས་པའི
ཁྱད་པར་དང། ཐོད་སྦྱན་དང་མངོན་ཤེས་ཆུམས་ལམ་དུས་ནས་རིམ
པར་ཇི་གསལ་ལ་སོང་བས་སངས་ཆུས་ཀྱི་སར་ཡོངས་ལུ་རྫོགས་པས
ཤིན་ཏུ་ཆུམ་པར་དག་ཅིང་མཐར་ཐུག་པ་སྟེ་ཡུལ་མ་ལུས་པ་ལ་ཆུ

divine eye, [bodhisattvas] can see the death, transition, and birth of every sentient being in the ten directions with their divine sight. (3) The wisdom eye is the wisdom that properly realizes nonself. (4) The dharma eye, according to Ācārya Vasubandhu, is comprised of nine out of ten strengths, excepting the strength of knowing what is appropriate and inappropriate. (5) The buddha eye is the realization of the complete perfection of all aspects of phenomena. These are the five eyes.

The six clairvoyances:

(1) The clairvoyance of miracles is the display of infinite miraculous apparitions. (2) The clairvoyance of divine ears is the ability to hear the sounds of infinite realms. (3) The clairvoyance of others' minds is knowledge of exactly what is occurring in the modality of the individual minds of all sentient beings. (4) [The clairvoyance of past existences is knowledge of the continuum of past and future lives of all individual sentient beings].[50] (5) The clairvoyance of the divine eye is the knowledge of the ways of birth and death, as well as the karmic causes and results, of all sentient beings. (6) The clairvoyance of the cessation of dissipation is their complete elimination through [knowing that] infinite obscurations are not present in essence.

The difference in the two divine eyes is that the former arises from karmic ripening, while the latter arises on the strength of meditation. In general, the eyes and clairvoyances are gradually clarified at the time of the path. Through that process, they are completely perfected on the level of a buddha. Then they are utterly pure and ultimate, such that one enters without limitation or bias or restrictions [into the knowledge of]

ཚད་ཕྱོགས་རིས་ཆགས་ཐོགས་མེད་པར་འཇུག་པ་སོགས་ཐུན་མོང་མིན་པ་ཉིད་དོ།།

སེམས་ཅན་སྨིན་པ་ནི། ཟས་སྨིན་ནས་བཟར་ཅང་བ་ལྟར་གདུལ་བྱ་རྣམས་སྦང་བྱ་སྦོང་ཅང་དང་གཉིན་པོ་རྣྲི་ཅང་དུ་སྨིན་པ་སྟེ། དཔེ་ན། བྱལ་བར་སྨིན་པ་སོགས་བརྒྱད་མདོ་རྒྱན་ལས་གསུངས་སོ། །ཞིང་སྐྱངས་པ་ནི། བཟང་སྡོད་ལས། གང་ཡང་དུས་གསུམ་དག་གི་ཞིང་བཀོད་པ། །དེ་དག་རྣལ་གཅིག་སྟེང་དུ་མངོན་པར་སྣྲུབ། །ཅེས་དང། ཞིང་རྣམས་རྒྱ་མཚོ་རྣམ་པར་དག་བྱེད་ཅིང། །ཞེས་པ་ལྟར་ཞིང་མཐའ་ཡས་སྣྲུབ་པ་དང་དེ་དག་བདེ་བ་ཅན་ལྟར་ཡོངས་སུ་དག་པར་སྦྱོང་བའོ། །ས་ངས་རྒྱས་ཀྱི་ཆོས་ནི། ས་ངས་རྒྱས་ཉིད་མ་གཏོགས་བྱང་སེམས་འཕགས་པས་ཀྱང་ཕྱོགས་ཙམ་ལས་མཚོན་མི་ནུས་པར་གསུངས་པས་བྱིས་པའི་བློའི་སྤྱོད་ཡུལ་ལས་འདས་མོད་ཀྱང་ཕྱོགས་སུ་བསྟུས་པ་ནི་གོང་ལྟར་སྣུ་དང་ཡེ་ཤེས་

all phenomena without exception, and so forth. Thus this is not in common [with those qualities at the time of the path].

Maturing sentient beings:

Just as food must be ripe to be edible, those to be trained are matured so that they are ready to eliminate what is to be eliminated and ready to develop the antidotes. There are eight divisions explicated in the *Adornment of the Sūtras*[51] and elsewhere, such as the maturing in freedom [from afflictions]. As for refining the realms, it says in the *Prayer of Samantabhadra's Conduct:*

> Whatever array of pure realms there are in the three times,
> they are all manifested upon a single atom.

And:

> [May I] totally purify an ocean of realms.[52]

Thus infinite realms are established and refined into total purity, like the Realm of Bliss (Sukhāvatī).

Buddha qualities:

It is said that other than a buddha, even the exalted bodhisattvas cannot demonstrate more than a fraction [of those qualities], so it is certainly beyond the intellectual sphere of childish people. Nevertheless, if one were to pose an approximate summary, it is said that they are subsumed into the

ཡོན་ཏན་ཕྱིན་ལས་རྣམས་ཀྱིས་ཉེ་བར་བསྡུས་པར་གསུངས་པས་
འདིར་ཡི་གེ་མང་ཕྱིར་མ་སྨོས་ཀྱང་བྱམས་ཆོས་ཆེ་བ་གསུམ་སོགས་
ལས་ཤེས་པར་བྱ་ཞིང་མདོ་ཙམ་བདེ་སྨོན་ཤེས་བྱའི་འགྲེལ་བར་ཡང་
གསལ་བོ། །ཞར་ཕྱུང་ལམ་གྱི་རིམ་པ་ཅུང་ཟད་སྨོས་ན། གྲུབ་ཆེན་
ནྱ་རོས་པས་ཕྱག་རྒྱ་ཆེན་པོ་ཚོག་བསྡུས་ལུ་གསུངས་པ་ལྟར་བརྒྱད་
པ་འདིའི་ཐུན་མོང་མ་ཡིན་པའི་ཆོས་སྐད་དུ་མཛད་པ་རྣལ་འབྱོར་
བཞི་རིམ་ནི། ཞི་གནས་ཀྱི་ས་མམས་རྩེ་གཅིག་པ་ཐོབ་ནས་གནས་པ་
ལ་ལྟག་མཐོང་ཤར་ཞིང་བདེ་གསལ་མི་རྟོག་པའི་ཉམས་འཁོར་ཡུག
ཏུ་འཕྱུང་བ་རྩེ་གཅིག་གི་རྣལ་འབྱོར་དང། སྣང་སེམས་ཀྱིས་བསྡུས
པའི་ཆོས་མཐའ་དག་ཆོས་དབྱིངས་བདེ་བ་ཆེན་པོའི་རང་བཞིན
ལས་མ་འདས་པར་མཐོང་བས་གཉིས་ཆོས་ཀྱི་སྒོས་འཛིན་ཐམས
ཅད་རང་གོལ་དུ་སོང་ཞིང་སྟོང་ཉིད་སྙིང་རྗེ་རྒྱུང་འཛུག་གི་ཡེ་ཤེས
ལྟག་མཐོང་མཚན་ཉིད་པ་ཐོབ་པས་ཞི་ལྟག་གི་རྣལ་འབྱོར་ཏི་ལྟ
བར་བྱང་དུ་ཚུད་པ་སྒོས་བབ་ཀྱི་རྣལ་འབྱོར་དང། དེ་གོང་ནས་གོང
དུ་གོམས་པས་ཆོས་ཐམས་ཅད་དུ་མ་རོ་གཅིག་ཏུ་རྟོགས་ཤིང་རྩོལ
མེད་ཀྱི་ཡེ་ཤེས་ནུས་པ་མེད་པར་སྣང་སེམས་དངོས་སུ་འདྲེས་པ་རོ
གཅིག་གི་རྣལ་འབྱོར་དང། བསྒོམས་པའི་འོད་གསལ་དང་གཞིའི
འོད་གསལ་གཅིག་ཏུ་འདྲེས་པས་གནས་ལུགས་ཀྱི་སྒྲིབ་གཡོག

kāyas, awarenesses, qualities, and enlightened activities that have been taught before. These will not be elaborated upon here for fear of too many words, but should be learned from the three great Maitreya Dharmas.[53] It is also clarified more succinctly in the commentary on the aspects to know in the *Aspiration Prayer for the Realm of Bliss*.[54]

Supplement: a brief description of the stages of the path

As the great adept Nāropa taught in *Concise Words on Mahāmudrā*,[55] this lineage employs an uncommon Dharma terminology, that of the four yogas.

(1) The yoga of single-pointed attention (*rtse gcig*): once the single-pointed focus of calm abiding is attained, higher insight arises within that state of abiding and the experiences of bliss, clarity, and nonthought arise all the time.

(2) The yoga free of elaboration (*spros bral*): by seeing that the whole range of phenomena that are appearing in the mind do not transcend the nature of the great bliss of the realm of phenomena, you are naturally liberated from all fixation on the dualistic elaborations regarding phenomena. You attain authentic higher insight, the unity of emptiness and compassion, and enter into the yoga where calm abiding and higher insight are properly unified.

(3) The yoga of one taste (*ro gcig*): As you become ever more familiarized with that, you realize that the multitude of all phenomena have but one taste. Appearance and mind are truly blended in the effortless gnosis that never declines.

(4) The yoga of nonmeditation (*sgom med*): The lucid clarity of meditation and the lucid clarity of the basic ground blend into one, by which all the obscurations that cover the

མཐའ་དག་གཞི་མེད་དུ་དྲངས། མཁྱམ་ཟླས་ཀྱི་མཚན་མས་ཞིག་ མཐར་ཐུག་གི་ཡོན་ཏན་ཐམས་ཅད་ལྷུན་གྱིས་ཏུ་འཕྲང་བ་སྣོམ་མེད་ཀྱི་ རྣལ་འབྱོར་ཞེས་བྱ་སྟེ། དེ་བཞི་ལ་ས་སོའི་མཚན་ཉིད་རྒྱལ་མ་ཟླ་གས་ པ་དང། ཕལ་ཆེར་ཟླ་གས་པ་དང། ཡོངས་སུ་ཟླ་གས་པའི་རིམ་པས་ ཚུང་འབྲིང་ཆེན་པོར་དབྱེ་བས་བཅུ་གཉིས་སུ་འགྱུར་ལ་དེ་དག་ཕར་ ཕྱིན་ཐེག་པའི་ལམ་དང་སྦྱར་ནས། རྒྱ་གཅིག་གསུམ་ཚོགས་ལམ། སྦྱོར་ བ་ལ་ཆུང་འབྲིང་སྦྱོར་ལམ། ཆེན་པོ་མཐོང་ལམ། རོ་གཅིག་གསུམ་ དང་སྒོམ་མེད་ཆུང་འབྲིང་སྒོམ་ལམ། སྒོམ་མེད་ཆེན་པོ་མཐར་ཕྱིན་ པའི་ལམ་དུ་གསུངས་པ་དང། ཡང་རྒྱུད་ཀྱི་དགོངས་པ་ཞེས་འགྲེལ་ ཐུན་དྲུག་རྣམས་ལས་གསུངས་པ་ལྟར་ཐུན་ལམ་ངེས་འབྱེད་ཏིང་ངེ་ འཛིན་གྱིས་ས་བཅུ་གཉིས་དང་སྦྱར་ནས་སྒོམ་མེད་ཆེན་པོ་མཐོང་ ལམ་དུ་བཞེད་པ་གཉིས་གདུལ་བྱའི་བློ་རིས་ལ་ལྟོས་ཏེ་དགོངས་གཞི་ དགོས་དབང་གིས་གསུངས་པའི་ཕྱིར། ངེས་པའི་དོན་གང་དུ་གནས་ ནི་མཁས་གྲུབ་ཆོས་སྐྱེན་ལྟར་པའི་ཞལ་གྱི་བདུད་རྩི་དངོས་སུ་ཐྱོང་ བ་དང། རྣལ་འབྱོར་རང་ཉིད་རྟོགས་གོམས་རབ་ཏུ་གྱུར་ཚེ་བསྒོམས་ ཟྱང་ཤེས་རབ་ཀྱིས་ངེས་པར་འགྱུར་བའོ།།

ཙ་བའི་ས་བཅད་གསུམ་པ་སྨོན་ལམ་གྱི་མཇུག་བསྡུ་བ་ལ་གཉིས། དངོས་དང། མཇུག་བྱང་བོ།།དང་པོ་ཀ་ངོས་ཀ་ནི།

abiding nature become transparent in their lack of a basis. The boundary between resting in equipoise and subsequent attainment vanishes. All the qualities of the ultimate state are spontaneously present.

Those four each have three levels: their attributes being underdeveloped, mostly developed, and fully developed—thus dividing into small, middle, and great—twelve stages in all. Compared with the paths of the Perfections Vehicle, it is taught that the three levels of single-pointed yoga correspond to the path of accumulation. The lesser and middle levels of freedom from elaboration correspond to the path of application, and the greater to the path of seeing. The three levels of one taste and the lesser level of nonmeditation are the path of meditation, and the greater level of nonmeditation corresponds to the ultimate path. Or, according to the intent of the tantras, *Bodhisattva Commentaries*,[56] and the six-branch yoga,[57] the absorption of definite discrimination on the path of application is associated with the twelve stages (*sa*; Skt. *bhūmi*), and the greater level of nonmeditation to the path of seeing. These two viewpoints depend upon the mental capacity of those to be trained, because they are taught out of the necessity to have a basis in Buddha's thought. As to where the definitive meaning lies, it will become certain by means of the wisdom from actually tasting the nectar from the mouths of those learned adepts with the eye of Dharma and from the result of meditation when the yogin truly attains excellent realization and familiarization.

III. Concluding summary of the aspiration

This has two parts: the main part and the colophon.

ཕྱོགས་བཅུའི་རྒྱལ་བ་སྲས་བཅས་ཐུགས་རྗེ་དང། །རྣམ་དཀར་དགེ་བ་ཇི་སྙེད་ཡོད་པའི་མཐུས། །དེ་ལྟར་བདག་དང་སེམས་ཅན་ཐམས་ཅད་ཀྱི། །སྨོན་ལམ་རྣམ་དག་ཇི་བཞིན་འགྲུབ་གྱུར་ཅིག

།ཅེས་གསུངས་ཏེ། ཕྱོགས་བཅུར་བཞུགས་པའི་རྒྱལ་བ་སྲས་དང་བཅས་པ་རྣམས་ཀྱི་དམིགས་པ་མེད་པའི་ཐུགས་རྗེ་ཆེན་པོ་དང། རྣམ་པར་དཀར་བའི་དགེ་བ་བཀྱིས་པ་དང་གཞན་ཀྱི་དགེ་བ་ལ་ཡི་རང་བཀྱིས་པ་ཇི་སྙེད་ཡོད་པའི་མཐུ་ལ་བརྟེན་ནས་དེ་ལྟར་འདིར་བསྡུན་ཀྱི་སྨོན་ལམ་ཉིད་གཙོར་བྱས་ནས་བདག་དང་སེམས་ཅན་ཐམས་ཅད་ཀྱི་སྨོན་ལམ་རྣམ་པར་དག་པ་ཇི་སྙེད་ཅིག་བཏབ་པ་དེ་ཐམས་ཅད་དེ་བཞིན་དུ་འགྲུབ་པར་གྱུར་ཅིག་ཅེས་པའོ། །

གཉིས་པ་ /མཇུག་བྱང་། ནི།

ངེས་དོན་ཕྱག་རྒྱ་ཆེན་པོའི་སྨོན་ལམ་ཞེས་བྱ་བ་རྗེ་རང་ཐུང་རྡོ་རྗེས་མཛད་པའོ།

།ཞེས་སོ། །དེ་ལྟར་དུས་གསུམ་རྒྱལ་བ་ཀུན་གྱི་བསྟོད་པ་གཅིག་པའི་ལམ་མཆོག མདོ་རྒྱུད་མན་ངག་ཐམས་ཅད་ཀྱི་བརྗོད་བྱ་མཐར་ཐུག ཀུན་པའི་ཐུན་མེས་མངའ་བསྟན་ཡབ་སྲས་ཀྱི་གདམས་ངག་རྫོགས་པའི་ས་ངས་རྒྱས་ཀྱི་བསྟུ་མེད་རྡོ་རྗེའི་ལུང་གིས་གསལ་བར་བསྟན་པ་བཞིན་དུ་མ་ཉམ་མེད་ཆོས་ཀྱི་རྒྱལ་པོ་དབུགས་པོ་ལྷ་རྗེས་རྒྱ་ཆེར་

A. Main part

25. *By the compassion of the ten-direction victors and their heirs,*
and the power of whatever pure virtue there is,
may my pure aspirations and those of all beings
all be fulfilled just as intended.

Based on **the** nonreferential great **compassion** of the **victors and their heirs** who dwell in **the ten directions**, and through **the power of whatever** totally **pure virtue** has been done and the rejoicing in whatever virtue **there is** that has been done by others, just like that, may whatever totally **pure aspirations** have been made by **me and all sentient beings**, headed mainly by this aspiration prayer that has been presented here, **all be fulfilled just as intended**.

B. Colophon

The Aspiration Prayer of Definitive Mahāmudrā *is by Lord Rangjung Dorjé.*

This is the single supreme path traveled by all the victors of the three times; the ultimate subject matter of all sutras, tantras, and esoteric instructions; and the instructions of the father–child lineage of the great ancestral adept, the Archer (Saraha). This doctrine, illuminated by the undeceiving vajra scriptures of the perfect Buddha, was exhaustively clarified by the unequaled king of Dharma, Dakpo Lhajé (Gampopa), and so it is the spiritual practice of the king of Kagyü adepts. This aspiration teaches clearly in a few summarized words the meaning of the ground,

གསལ་བར་མཛད་པས་བཀའ་བཀྲྀད་གྱི་ཐོག་རྒྱལ་པོའི་ཐུགས་
དམ་ཅེས་དོན་ཕྱག་རྒྱ་ཆེན་པོར་གྱུགས་པའི་གཞི་ལམ་འབྲས་གསུམ་
གྱི་དོན་རྣམས་ཚོག་ཏུང་འདུས་ཀྱིས་གསལ་བར་སྟོན་པའི་སྟོན་ལམ་
འདི་ཉིད། བདག་ཅག་གི་འདྲེན་པ་བྱུག་པ་སེམ་ཕྲེའི་རྣམ་པར་རོལ་པ་
ཐམས་ཅད་མཁྱེན་པ་དཔལ་ལྡན་ཀརྨ་པ་རང་ཐུང་རྗེ་རྗེའི་ཞལ་སྔ·
ནས་ཀྱིས་རྗེས་འཇུག་རྣམས་ལ་ཐུགས་བརྩེ་བས་གདམས་པའི་ཕྱིར·
ནན་ཏན་དུ་འབད་པར་གཅེས་ཏེ། ཀུན་མཁྱེན་མི་བསྟོད་རྗེ་རྗེའི·
ཞལ་ནས། ཆོས་ཚུལ་འདི་ལ་བཀའ་བཀྲྀད་འདི་པ་ཐུགས་ཅེས་པོ·
ཆེར་བཟུང་ནས་དམ་ཆོས་བླ་ན་མེད་པར་མཛད་པས། སྐལ་ལྡན་ཀྱི·
སྐྱེ་བུ་དག ར་བ་རྒྱགས་པ། འཕྲིང་ཁམས། མཐའ་མཀའ་ཁོ་བའི་ཤེས·
ར་ཅམ་ཀྱིས་ཀྱང་ཁམས་ནུ་ཅི་ལོང་ལ་འབད་པར་ཀྱིས་ཤེག་ཅེས·
འདོམས་པར་མཛད་དོ། །ངེས་དོན་ཟབ་མོའི་ཚུལ་ལ་དང་འདོད·
ཡིད་ཆེས་ཀྱི་དད་པས་འཇུག་པ་ལྟ་ཅི་སྟོས། ཐོས་ནས་ཡིད་མ་ཆེས·
པར་ཐེ་ཚོམ་དུ་གྱུར་པ་རྣམས་ཀྱང་ཐེ་ཚོམ་གྱི་ཉེས་པས་རེ་ཞིག་ངན·
ས྅ོར་སོང་ཡང། ཟབ་དོན་ཐོས་པའི་ཏིན་མཐུས་ཡུན་མི་རིང་བར་དེ·
ལས་ཐར་ནས་བྱང་ཆུབ་འཐོབ་པར་སངས་རྒྱས་ཀྱིས་ལུང་བསྟན·
བསྟལ་བའི་ལོ་རྒྱས་དུ་མ་མདོ་ཐེ་རྣམས་ལས་འབྱུང་ཞིང། ཟློབ·
དཔོན་ཀླུ་ཞབས་ཀྱིས་ཀྱང། བསོད་ནམས་ཆུང་བས་ཆོས་འདི་ལ། ཐེ·
ཚོམ་ཅམ་ཡང་མི་སྐྱེ་སྟེ། །འདི་ལ་ཐེ་ཚོམ་སྐྱེས་པས་ཀྱང། །ཁྱིད་པ·
ཏྲལ་པོར་བྱེད་པར་འགྱུར། །ཞེས་གསུངས་ཤིང་དད་པ་གསུམ་ཀྱིས·
འབད་པའི་ཕན་ཡོན་ནི། འདི་དང་མ་འབྲེལ་བའི་དགེ་བ་རྒྱ་ཆེན·
པོ་བསྐལ་པ་གང་གཱའི་ཀླུང་གི་བྱེ་སྟེད་དུ་བསྒྲུབ་པའི་བསོད་ནམས·

path, and fruition of the renowned definitive mahāmudrā. Our guide, the [future] sixth lion emanation,[58] omniscient glorious Karmapa Rangjung Dorjé, spoke this instruction out of love for future followers. Therefore, cherish it and strive in persistent practice. The all-knowing Mikyö Dorjé counseled:

> In this Dharma system, this Kagyüpa, [when you] deeply appreciate its great value, you make it the unsurpassable holy Dharma. Then, the best of the fortunate disciples will have realization, the average will have experiences, and even the least of them will gain at least the wisdom of understanding. Whatever you take into practice, preserver in it.[59]

There is no need to discuss those who possess enthusiastic, longing, and confident faith in this profound system of the definitive meaning. Even those flawed doubters who hear it but don't believe it will go to the lower realms for a while, but not for very long. The power of the blessings of hearing the profound meaning will liberate them from there and they will gain enlightenment. There are many such stories of prophesies by the Buddha in the sutras. Also, Master Nāgārjuna said,

> Those of little merit will not doubt this Dharma.
> But even if they do, it will still shred existence.[60]

Regarding the benefits of exerting yourself with the three kinds of faith, there is greater benefit in hearing the mere words and developing interest and confidence in this kind of Dharma that teaches the abiding nature of suchness than in

ལས་ཀྱང། བསམ་གྱིས་མི་ཁྱབ་པ་དེ་ཁོ་ན་ཉིད་ཀྱི་གནས་ལུགས་སྟོན་
པའི་ཆོས་ཚུལ་འདི་ལྟ་བུའི་ཚིག་ཙམ་ཐོས་ནས་མོས་པ་དང་ལྡན་
པས་ཡིད་ཆེས་ན་ཕན་ཡོན་ཆེ་བར་བཀའ་དང་བསྟན་བཅོས་རྣམས་
ལས་རྒྱ་ཆེར་གསུངས་སོ། །མདོ་རྒྱུད་མན་ངག་ཟབ་དོན་ཀུན་དང་
མཐུན། །ཕྱིན་ཆད་བདག་ཀྱིས་ཀུན་ལས་ཁྱད་པར་འཕགས། །དད་
བཙོན་ཤེར་གསུམ་ལྡན་པ་ལྟ་ཅི་སྨོས། །ཚོངས་རྒྱལ་མོས་གུས་དྲག
པོས་འབད་ཏུས་ཀྱང། །སྲིད་མཚོ་ཆེ་གྲེས་ཆུ་ཙམ་བྱེད་པ་ནི། །རྡོ་རྗེ
འཛིན་ནས་ཀུ་བའི་བློ་མའི་བར། །རྟོགས་པ་དོན་གྱི་བརྒྱུད་པ་མ་ཆད
པས། །ཆུ་བརྒྱུད་བློ་མའི་ཕྱིན་ཆད་ཁོ་ནའི་མཐུ། །དེ་ཕྱིར་འདི་སྐྱོང
ཤེལ་པ་ལྟན་དུས་འདིར། །མི་དབང་རིན་ཆེན་བདུན་དང་དཔལ
འབྱོར་ཀྱང། །ཆུ་ཤིང་འདྲ་བར་གསུངས་ན་ཁྱོག་ཁུག་གཞི། །ཚེ་འདིའི
བྱ་བ་འཇིག་བརྟེན་ཆོས་བརྒྱུད་པོ། །ཆུ་ལྟར་དོར་ནས་ཆོག་ཤེས་ཁོར
ལྟན་པས། །བརྒྱུད་པ་འདི་ཡི་གདུང་རབས་མི་གཅོད་ནི། །སྒྲུབ་པའི
གཙོ་བོ་བླ་མ་སྒྲུབ་པ་དང། །མཆོད་པའི་གཙོ་བོ་བླ་མ་མཆོད་པ་དང
།ཉམས་ལེན་གཙོ་བོ་གསོལ་བ་འདེབས་པ་ལ། །ཀྱིས་ཞེས་བཀའ
བརྒྱུད་གོང་མའི་གསུངས་པ་ལྟར། །རྩེ་གཅིག་སྒྲུབ་ལ་འབད་ན་ཅིས
མི་འཚོང། །མདོ་རྒྱུད་ལུང་དང་གྲུབ་པའི་ཞལ་བཞེས་ལགས།

the merit of accomplishing vast amounts of virtue for as many eons as there are sands of the River Ganges without this connection. So it is taught extensively in the Buddhist scriptures and treatises.

In accord with all profound meanings in sutra, tantra, and upadeśa,
this is especially exalted over all by the descent of blessings.
If the dull-witted endeavor with intense devotion,
let alone those with faith, diligence, and wisdom,
the ocean of existence will shrink to the water in a footprint.
Since the lineage of genuine realization is unbroken
from Vajradhara down to the root guru,
the power of the root and lineage gurus' blessing suffices.
Therefore the activity of fortunate ones is now.
Since even the seven jewels and the wealth of a ruler
are said to be like a hollow plantain tree, they are bases of evil and suffering.
Discard this life's deeds and eight worldly concerns
like roots and gain the wealth of contentment.
In the legacy of this uninterrupted lineage,
the principal practice is the guru practice,
the principal offering is the guru offering,
the principal application is supplication.
So as the previous Kagyü masters said: "Do it!"
If you strive in practice with single focus, why wouldn't you thrive?
That is the promise of the sutras, tantras, transmissions, and adepts.

།བཀྲུད་པ་འདི་དང་གདམས་པ་འདི་ཉིད་ལ། །ལྷན་སྐྱེས་དང་པས་
ཕྱག་ཙམ་མཚོན་པར་བྱས། །བྱིས་བློའི་དབང་གིས་ནོངས་པའི་
ཚོགས་མ་ལུས། །ཐོག་མེད་ཉེས་ལྡང་རྣམས་དང་ཆབས་ཅིག་ཏུ། །རྩ
བ་བཀྲུད་པའི་དཔལ་ལྷན་བློ་མར་བཤགས། །རྣམ་དཀར་མཆིས་ན
བདག་གཞན་འཕེལ་ཐོགས་མཚོན། །མཁའ་མཉམ་ཡིད་ཅན་མ་ལུས
ཕྱག་རྒྱ་ཆེའི། །གོ་འཕང་རྩོལ་མེད་འཐོབ་པའི་རྒྱ་ཀུར་ཅིག །ཅེས་པ
འདིའང་དུས་འཁོར་ཕྱིས་ལུགས་དཔལ་རང་བྱང་ཞབས་ཀྱིས་བཞེད
པས། བདག་ཅག་གི་སྟོན་པ་ཐུབ་པའི་དབང་པོ་ས་ཁྱི་ལོར་མངོན
པར་སངས་རྒྱས་ཏེ་ཆོས་འཁོར་བསྐོར་ནས་བགྲང་བ་ཉིས་སྟོང
བཀྲད་བཀྲ་བཅོ་བཀྲད་པ་ཤིང་ལུགས་ས་གา་ཟླ་བའི་དཀར་ཕྱོགས་དགེ
བར། ཕྱག་ན་པདྨོ་དཔལ་ཀན্ས་ཀ་ཡབ་སྲས་ཀྱི་ཞབས་རྡུལ་ཐྲི་བོར
རེག་པའི་བན་ཏན་མ་ཅི་བ་ངེས་དོན་བསྟན་རྒྱས་པས་ཀུན་གཟིགས
བསྟན་པའི་ཉིན་བྱེད་ཀྱི་གསུང་གི་སྣང་བ་ལ་བརྟེན་ནས་ཟླུང་ཆེན
དལ་འབབ་ཀྱི་འགྲམ་ངོགས་འོད་གསལ་ཐང་གི་དབེན་པར་གཅིག
པུར་གནས་སྐབས་རང་གི་བརྩེད་བྱང་དུ་སྲུག་རིས་ལུ་བསྟར་བ་དགེ
ལེགས་འཕེལ། ས་ཕ་མཆ་ལོ།། ||

With spontaneous faith in this lineage and this instruction,
I have gestured in the direction [of its meaning],
but due to my immature intellect, it is full of mistakes.
This, together with all faults and failings since beginningless time,
I acknowledge before the glorious root and lineage gurus.
If there is anything good, may it cause myself and others connected with it,
and by extension all sentient beings throughout space,
to effortlessly attain the state of mahāmudrā.

According to the date calculations in the *Kālacakra Tantra*, to which the glorious Venerable Rangjung adhered, from the time our Teacher Śākyamuni manifested buddhahood in the earth dog year and turned the wheel of the Dharma, it is calculated to be 2818. In the virtue of the full moon of the [fourth] month (*vaiśākha*) of the wood sheep year (1895), touching to my head the dust beneath the feet of the lotus-holding glorious succession of Karmapas, this old *maṇi*-mumbling monk composed this as a memorandum to myself based on the teachings of Kunzik Situ Tenpai Nyinjé's exhaustively-presented definitive meaning, while staying alone in the isolated place of radiant white sand on the banks of a slowly flowing river.

May virtue flourish.

Sarva maṅgalaṃ

Notes

1. Karma Rinchen Dargyé, *Excellent Vase of Elixir* (*Nges don phyag rgya chen po'i smon lam gyi 'grel chung bdud rtsi'i bum bzang*).
2. Gray, "Imprints of the 'Great Seal,'" 425.
3. *Phyag ni ston pa'i ye shes / rgya ni de las mi 'da' bas / chen po gong na med pa'o.* I wrote this down from the retreat master Lama Tenpa so long ago that I have forgotten the source.
4. Situ Tenpai Nyinjé, *Oral Transmission of the Supreme Siddhas*, 68; quoting from Vajrapāṇi, *Instructions from the Successive Guru Lineage*, 179a2.
5. See Dalton, "Mahāmudrā and Samayamudrā in the Dunhuang Documents and Beyond."
6. Roberts, *Mind of Mahāmudrā*, 3. See Roger Jackson's translations of dohās from the original Apabhraṃśa language in *Tantric Treasures*.
7. Dakpo Tashi Namgyal, *Phyag chen zla ba'i 'od zer*, ff.108b–110b.
8. Jamgön Kongtrul, *Treasury of Knowledge, Book 8, Part 4: Esoteric Instructions*, 138–39.
9. *Sdom gsum rab dbye*, translated by Jared Rhoton as *A Clear Differentiation of the Three Codes*.

10. Jamgön Kongtrul, *Treasury of Knowledge, Book 8, Part Four: Esoteric Instructions*, 212.
11. Jared Rhoton put the first documented written reply to a few passages as coming from the fourth Shamar, Chökyi Drakpa (1453–1524), some two and a half centuries later.
12. See for example Gorampa Sönam Sengé, *Complete Explanation of A Clear Differentiation of the Three Codes*.
13. See my research in an unpublished paper, "As for the Blessing of Vajravārāhī, Marpa Lhodrakpa Does Not Have It."
14. Mathes, "Blending the Sūtras with the Tantras," 225.
15. *Sdom gsum rab dbye'i spyi ti ga byed pa bdag thang chad do*. In Padma Karpo, *Pith of Dharma*, 4–5.
16. Roberts, *Mind of Mahāmudrā*, 9.
17. Thanks to Dolma Khyab for his help clarifying this story.
18. Liberation through seeing, hearing, recalling, and touching.
19. *Array of Qualities in Mañjuśrī's Buddha Realm*, 279a. The last line in the Kangyur reads *de 'dre'i 'bras bu thob par 'gyur*, but the meaning is the same.
20. Aśvaghoṣa II, *Gurupañcāśikā*, 10a2–12a2.
21. The six limits and the four modes (*mtha' drug tshul bzhi*), the indispensable keys for unlocking the meaning of the tantras. The six limits are the views of the (1) expedient meaning (*drang don*), (2) definitive meaning (*nges don*), (3) implied (*dgongs pa can*), (4) not implied (*dgongs pa can ma yin pa*), (5) literal (*sgra ji bzhin pa*), and (6) not literal (*sgra ji bzhin ma yin pa*). The four modes

(*tshul bzhi*) are the (1) literal (*tshig*), (2) general (*spyi*), (3) hidden (*sbas*), and the (4) ultimate (*mthar thug*).

22. Nāgārjuna, *In Praise of Dharmadhātu*, verse 17, 64a7.
23. *Sems yid rnam shes*, although *sems* is usually understood as "mind" or "mental consciousness," here, according to Ācārya Lama Tenpa, it refers to the all-ground consciousness.
24. Maitreyanātha, *Mahāyānottaratantraśāstra*, or *Uttaratantraśāstra* 54b1–45a6.
25. Constituent (*khams*; Skt. *dhātu*) in this context is used as a synonym for the essence or potential for being buddha (Skt: *tathāgatagarbha*), commonly referred to as "buddha nature."
26. Nāgārjuna, *In Praise of Dharmadhātu*, verse 11, 64a3. Following the Tengyur edition, the last line should read *nyon mongs 'ba' zhig bskyed par zad* rather than *ngal ba 'ba' zhig skyed par zad* ("effort generates nothing but exhaustion").
27. *Zung 'jug rab tu mi gnas pa'i dbu ma*. Of the seemingly vast classifications of Madhyamaka, there are two schools called "those who logically establish illusion" (*sgyu ma rigs grub pa*) and "proponents of total nonabiding" (*rab tu mi gnas par smra ba*). Jamgön Kongtrul, *The Treasury of Knowledge, Book 6, Part 3: Frameworks of Buddhist Philosophy*, 367–68, n617. A further division into "four kinds of nonabiding" consists of the total nonabiding of emptiness, the total nonabiding of severed continuity, the total nonabiding of equanimity, and the total nonabiding of unity. See Brunnhölzl, *Center of the Sunlit Sky*, all of chapter 3.

28. *Mtha' bral.* A note about this ubiquitous term "free of extremes." Although it indicates so-called extremes of believing in the permanence of objects or a kind of nihilism, it is not just these extremes but virtually any kind of reference point at all, for even a centrist position can be a reference.
29. Not a sutra but a treatise by Jñānagarbha, *Distinguishing the Two Truths*, 2a4–5.
30. A reference to Situ Tenpai Nyinjé's commentary on the same text. See Situ Tenpai Nyinjé, *Oral Transmission of the Supreme Siddhas*, 225–28. Compared to the rest of Situ's commentary, this section *is* rather short.
31. Nāgārjuna, *Root Verses on the Middle Way Called Wisdom*, chap. 24, verse 18, 15a6.
32. *Ḍākinī Vajra Tent Tantra,* chap. 6, 44a4. There, *gang zag* ("persons") replaces *sems can* ("sentient beings"). For context, the last two lines of the verse are: "The abiding meaning of consciousness, or not something external" (*rnam par shes pa'i gnas don nam / phyi rol gyur pa yod ma yin*).
33. Saraha, *Songs of the Dohā Treasury*, 72b5. This particular quotation comes from the dohā known as "The People's Dohā" in Saraha's trilogy of advice to the king, the queen, and the people.
34. Saraha, *Dohā Treasury of Mahāmudrā Instructions*, 123b2.
35. Although here attributed to Nāgārjuna, it is found in Maitreyanātha, *Distinguishing the Middle from the Extremes*, chap. 1, 40b4, with slight variations. It is also quoted in *Kagyü Mahāmudrā Dharma Cycle*, where it is attributed to *Secret Lamp Tantra* (*Gsang ba'i sgron me'i*

rgyud). The full citation reads: "Through relying on the reference points / the nonreferential itself will fully emerge. / When accustomed to the nonreferential, / the essence of the nonreferential is achieved."

36. The gloss here refers to Nāgārjuna's *Suhṛllekha*, 42b6. The passage there has been translated by the Padmakara Translation Group as "Wildness and remorse, and hateful thoughts, / And dullness-somnolence, and yearning lust, / And doubt are hindrances—please know these five / Are thieves that steal the gem of virtuous deeds." See *Nagarjuna's Letter to a Friend*, 108.
37. *'Du byed brgyad*. The eight remedies are aspiration or interest (*mos pa*), exertion (*rtsol ba*), faith (*dad pa*), flexibility (*shin sbyangs*), recollection or mindfulness (*dran pa*), awareness (*shes bzhin*), attention (*sems pa*), and equanimity (*shes bzhin*).
38. *Sems dgu* (*sems zhi bar gnas pa'i thabs dgu*). The nine techniques of mental calm abiding are: mental placement (*sems 'jog pa*), constant placement (*rgyun du 'jog pa*), integrated placement (*glan te 'jog pa*), intensified placement (*nye bar 'jog pa*), control (*'dul ba*), calmness (*zhi ba*), quiescence (*rnam par zhi ba*), one-pointedness (*rtse gcig*), and equipoise (*mnyam par 'jog pa*). See Jamgön Kongtrul, *Treasury of Knowledge, Book 6, Parts 1 and 2: Indo-Tibetan Classical Learning and Buddhist Phenomenology*, 428–29.
39. *Zhi byed* (*zhijé*) or the longer name *Sdug bsngal zhi byed* ("Pacification of Suffering") is a general name for the extensive corpus of instructions attributed to the Indian adept called Dampa Sangyé (or Kamalaśrī/Kamālaśīla), and also the name of his lineage or school. See Jamgön

Kongtrul, *Treasury of Precious Instructions, Volume 13: Zhije.*

40. *Gcod* (*chöd*) means to sever, cut, or determine, and refers to the widespread practice developed by the Tibetan yoginī Machik Lapdrön. However, the line here is open to some interpretation; given the long list of named practices in this passage, I regard it as a reference to the Chöd practice of "cutting" negative forces. Another version by Peter Alan Roberts reads "It was taught that even obstacles / from demons, māras, and so on should be exalted." Roberts, *Mahāmudrā and Related Instructions*, 252.
41. From Pakmo Drupa, *Applied Coemergence*, 258–59. This is part of an explanation of the term *lhan cig skyes sbyor* (Skt. *sahaja* or *sahajayoga*), sometimes translated as "connate union." The reproduction here seems to have left important lines out, so I have added the lines missing from there. There are also two important differences: "instructions on valid cognition" (*tshad mai'i gdams ngag*) rather than "guru's instruction" and "joined as/in mind by instructions" (*gdams pas sems su sbyor*) rather than "joined as one." Also Pakmo Drupa attributes this as being "from the mouth of the Lord," presumably his guru Gampopa Sönam Rinchen.
42. Unknown reference. Possibly Rāga Asya, also known as Karma Chakmé.
43. Advayavajra, *Scriptural Commentary on the Songs of the Dohā Treasury*, 198b5.
44. *Rtags bcu*. The ten signs of lucid clarity are: smoke, mirage, clouds, fireflies, sun, moon, shining jewels,

eclipse, stars, and light rays. Roberts, *Mahāmudrā and Related Instructions*, 639, n223.

45. This has not been located in a sutra, but is quoted in many sources, such as Gampopa's *Jewel Ornament of Liberation,* 40b4.
46. Nāgārjuna, *Commentary on Awakening Mind*, verse 2, 41a3.
47. The quotation appears in several places in Gampopa's *Collected Works*, such as *Garland of Pearls*, 12a.
48. Nāgārjuna, *Commentary on Awakening Mind*, 41b3.
49. *Bhu su ku*, or *bu su ku*, an Indian word referring to ordinary daily functions, specifically eating (*bha*), sleeping (*su*), and walking (*ku*). In other words, the yogic conduct of practicing nothing but the basics.
50. This is missing from Mendong Tsampa's commentary and has been added from Situ Tenpai Nyinjé, *Oral Transmission of the Supreme Siddhas*: *bzhi pa sngon gnas rjes dran gyi mngon shes / sems can thams cad kyi so so'i 'das pa dang ma 'ongs pa'i skye ba brgyud mar shes pa.*
51. Maitreyanātha, *Ornament of the Mahāyāna Sutras,* 40b1–45a6.
52. *Āryabhadracaryāpraṇidhānarāja*, 264b2–3 and 264b7. Also known as *Prayer of Excellent Conduct*, this immensely popular prayer is based on a passage in the final part of the *Avataṃsaka Sūtra*. It stands on its own in the *dhāraṇī* section of the Kangyur.
53. The first three of the five treatises (*Byams chos lnga*) composed by Asaṅga and attributed to Maitreya: *Ornament of Clear Realization, Ornament of the Mahāyāna Sutras, Mahāyāna Highest Continuum, Distinguishing Dharma*

from Dharmatā, and *Distinguishing the Middle from the Extremes*.

54. *Bde ba can kyi smon lam* or *Chags med bde smon*, Karma Chakmé's famous prayer based on the Sukhāvatī Sutras. Mendong Tsampa himself composed a commentary to this prayer called *Swift Travel to the Pure Realm: A Short Commentary on the Aspiration Prayer of the Realm of Bliss*, 308–402.
55. *Phyag rgya chen po tshig bsdus* (**Mahāmudrāsaṅcamitha*). Not in the Tengyur. The two-folia text by this name is in Jamgön Kongtrul, *Treasury of Precious Instructions* (vol. 7, 47–48), and does not mention the four yogas.
56. *Trilogy of Bodhisattva Commentaries*.
57. *Sbyor drug* (Skt. *ṣaḍaṅgayoga*), the six-branch yoga in the tradition of the *Kālacakra Tantra*.
58. According to the *Fortunate Eon Sutra*, one thousand buddhas will appear in this eon. Śākyamuni was the fourth, Maitreya the fifth, and the sixth will be Siṁha (Seng ge, "Lion"). This will be the successor currently known as Karmapa.
59. From Mikyö Dorjé, *Collection of Advice on Mahāmudrā*. There, it begins with "conceptual thoughts as dharmakāya and appearances as one's own mind, in this Dharma system" (*rnam rtog chos kyi sku dang snang ba rang gi sems zhes*).
60. Although attributed here to Nāgārjuna, and specifically to *Precious Garland [A Letter to the King]* by Tai Situ Tenpai Nyinjé, it is actually found in Āryadeva, *Four Hundred Verse Treatise*, 9a7. Apparently a different translation was used here.

Bibliography

Kangyur (Canonical Scriptures)

Array of Qualities in Mañjuśrī's Buddha Realm. Mañjuśribuddhakṣetraguṇavyūha. 'Jam dpal gyi sangs rgyas kyi zhing gi yon tan bkod pa. Toh 59, dkon brtsegs, *ga*, 248b1–297a3.

Ḍākinī Vajra Tent Tantra. Ḍākinīvajrapañjarātantra. Mka' 'gro ma rdo rje gur zhes bya ba'i rgyud kyi rgyal po chen po'i brtag pa. Toh 419, rgyud, *nga*, 30a4–65b7.

Fortunate Eon Sutra. Bhadrakalpikasūtra. Bskal pa bzang po'i mdo. Toh 94, mdo sde, *ka*, 1b1–340a5.

Prayer of Samantabhadra's Conduct. Āryabhadracaryāpraṇidhānarāja. 'Phags pa bzang po spyod pa'i smon lam gyi rgyal po. Toh 1095, gzung 'dus, *wam*, 262b3–266a3.

Tengyur (Canonical Treatises)

Advayavajra (Gnyis su med pa'i rdo rje). *Scriptural Commentary on the Songs of the Dohā Treasury. Dohākoṣapañjikā. Do ha mdzod kyi dka' 'grel.* Toh 2256, rgyud, *wi*, 180b3–207a7.

Āryadeva. *The Four Hundred Verse Treatise. Catuḥśatakaśāstra. Bstan bcos bzhi brgya pa zhes bya ba'i tshig le'ur byas pa.* Toh 3846, dbu ma, *tsha*, 1a1–18a7.

Aśvaghoṣa II (Rta dbyangs, 10th century). *Fifty Verses of Guru Devotion. Gurupañcāśikā. Bla ma lnga bcu pa.* Toh 3721, rgyud, *tshu*, 10a2–12a2.

Jñānagarbha. *Distinguishing the Two Truths. Satyadvayavibhaṅgakārikā. Bden pa gnyis rnam par 'byed pa'i tshig le'ur byas pa.* Toh 3881, dbu ma, *sa*, 1b–3b.

Maitreyanātha. *Distinguishing Dharma from Dharmatā. Dharmadharmatāvibhāga. Chos dang chos nyid rnam par 'byed pa.* Toh 4022, sems tsam, *phi*, 46b–49a.

———. *Distinguishing the Middle from the Extremes. Madhyāntavibhāga. Dbus dang mtha' rnam par 'byed pa'i tshig le'u byas pa.* Toh 4021, sems tsam, *phi*, 40b1–45a6.

———. *Mahāyāna Highest Continuum. Ratnagotravibhāga Mahāyānottaratantraśāstra. Theg pa chen po rgyud bla ma'i bstan bcos.* Toh 4024, sems tsam, *phi*, 54b1–45a6.

———. *Ornament of Clear Realization. Abhisamayālaṃkāra. Mngon par rtogs pa'i rgyan.* Toh 3786, shes phyin, *ka*, 1b–13a.

———. *Ornament of the Mahāyāna Sutras. Mahāyānosūtrālaṃkāra. Mdo sde brgyan.* Toh 4020, sems tsam, *phi*, 1a1–39a4.

Nāgārjuna. *Commentary on Awakening Mind. Bodhicittavivaraṇa. Byang chub sems 'grel.* Toh 1800, rgyud, *ngi*, 41a1–42b5.

———. *Letter to a Friend. Suhṛllekha. Bshes pa'i spring yig.* Toh 4182, spring yig, *nge*, 40b4–46b3.

———. *In Praise of Dharmadhātu. Dharmadhātustava. Chos kyi byings su bstod pa.* Toh 1118, bstod tshogs, *ka*, 63b5–67b3.

———. *Root Verses on the Middle Way Called Wisdom. Prajñānāmamūlamadhyamakakārikā. Dbu ma rtsa ba'i tshig le'ur byas pa shes rab ces bya ba.* Toh 3824, dbu ma, *tsa*, 1a1–19a6.

Saraha. *Dohā Treasury of Mahāmudrā Instructions. Dohākoṣanāma mahāmudropadeśa. Do ha mdzod ces bya ba phyag rgya chen po'i man ngag.* Toh 2273, rgyud, *zhi*, 122a3–124a7.

———. *Songs of the Dohā Treasury. Dohākoṣagīti. Do ha mdzod kyi glu.* Toh 2224, rgyud, *wi*, 70b5–77a3.

Trilogy of Bodhisattva Commentaries. Sems 'grel skor gsum. One each by Puṇḍarīka, Vajragarbha, and Vajrapāṇi, focusing on the *Kālacakra, Hevajra,* and *Cakrasaṃvara* tantras, respectively. Toh 1347, 1180, and 1402.

Vajrapāṇi. *Instructions from the Successive Guru Lineage. Guruparaṃparakramapadeśa. Bla ma brgyud pa'i rim pa'i man ngag.* Toh 3716, rgyud, *tsu*, 164b2–183a5.

Tibetan Works

Bokar Tulku, Karma Ngedön Chökyi Lodrö ('Bo dkar sprul sku Karma nges don chos kyi blo gros). *Lamp for the Minds of the Faithful: A Rough Sketch of the Activities of the Glorious Guru. Dpal ldan bla ma'i mdzad rnam rag bsdus mos ldan yid kyi sgron me.* In *Collected Works of Mendong Tsampa Rinpoché*, vol. 3, 490–500.

Collected Works of Mendong Tsampa Rinpoché, Karma Ngedön Tengyé. 3 vols. Reproduced from tracings from the collected block prints impressed from the xylographs preserved at Sman Dgon Thub-chen-bde-chen-gling. Bir, HP: D. Tsondu Senghe, 1975.

Dakpo Tashi Namgyal (Dwags po Bkra shis rnam rgyal). *Moonbeams of Mahāmudrā. Phyag chen zla ba'i 'od zer.* Tibetan xylograph edition. Sikkim: Rumtek Monastery, n.d.

Gampopa Sönam Rinchen (Gam po pa Bsod nams rin chen). *Collected Works of Gampopa Sönam Rinchen*. 4 vols. Kathmandu: Khenpo S. Tenzin and Lama T. Namgyal, 2000. BDRC W23439.

———. *Garland of Pearls: A Teaching for the Assembly. Tshogs chos mu tig gi phreng ba*. In *Collected Works of Gampopa Sönam Rinchen*, vol. 1, 577–669.

———. *Jewel Ornament of Liberation. Dam chos yid bzhin nor bu thar pa rin po che'i rgyan*. In *Collected Works of Gampopa Sönam Rinchen*, vol. 4, 193–660.

Gorampa Sönam Sengé (Go ram pa Bsod nams seng ge). *Complete Explanation of A Clear Differentiation of the Three Codes, Clarifying the Intention of the Victor's Speech. Sdom pa gsum gyi rab tu dbye ba'i rnam bshad rgyal ba'i gsung rab kyi dgong pa gsal ba*. In *The Collected Works of Kun-mkyen Go-rams-pa bsod-nams-seng-ge*, vol. 9. Dehra Dun: Sakya College, 1979. BDRC W11249-0439.

Kagyü Mahāmudrā Dharma Cycle. Bka' brgyud pa'i phyag chen chos skor. Swayambhu, Kathmandu: Karma Lekshey Ling, 2012. BDRC W3JT13326.

Karma Rinchen Dargyé (Karma Rin chen dar rgyas). *Excellent Vase of Elixir: Short Commentary on the Aspiration Prayer of Definitive Mahāmudrā. Nges don phyag rgya chen po'i smon lam gyi 'grel chung bdud rtsi'i bum bzang.* Swayambu, Kathmandu: Karma Lekshey Ling, 2012. BDRC W3JT13321.

Mendong Tsampa, Karma Ngedön Tengyé (Sman sdong mtshams pa, Karma nges don bstan rgyas). *Collected Works of Mendong Tsampa Rinpoché*. 3 vols. Bir, HP: D. Tsondu Senghe, 1975.

———. *Ornament of Dakpo Kagyü Thought: A Short Commentary on the Mahāmudrā Aspiration Prayer. Phyag chen smon lam 'grel chung dwags brgyud dgongs rgyan*. In *Collected Works of Mendong Tsampa Rinpoché*, vol. 1, 403–74.

———. *Swift Travel to the Pure Realm: A Short Commentary on the Aspiration Prayer of the Realm of Bliss. Bde smon 'grel chung zhing khams myur bgrod*. In *Collected Works of Mendong Tsampa Rinpoché*, vol. 1, 308–402.

Mikyö Dorjé (Mi bskyod rdo rje), the eighth Karmapa. *Collection of Advice on Mahāmudrā. Phyag rgya chen po sgros 'bum*. In *Collected Works of Karma pa Mi bskyod rdo rje*, vol. 24, 3–468. Lhasa, 2004. BDRC W8039.

Nāropa. *Concise Words on Mahāmudrā. *Mahāmudrāsañcamitha. Phyag rgya chen po tshig bsdus*. Included in Jamgön Kongtrul's compiled *Treasury of Precious Instructions*, vol. 7, 47–48. (Not in the Tengyur.)

Pakmo Drupa (Phag mo gru pa). *Applied Coemergence. Lhan cig skyes sbyor*. In *Collected Works of Pakmo Drupa*, vol. *nga* (4), 256–82. Kathmandu: Khenpo S. Tenzin and Lama T. Namgyal, 2003.

Padma Karpo (Padma dkar po). *The Pith of Dharma: Complete Explanation of the Bodiless Ḍākinī. Lus med mkha' 'gro'i chos sde'i rnam par bshad pa chos kyi nying khu*. In *Collected Works of Kun mkhyen Padma dkar po*. Darjeeling: Kargyud Sungrab Nyamso Khang, 1973–74. BDRC W10736.

Rāga Asya [Karma Chakmé]. *Aspiration Prayer for the Realm of Bliss. Chags med bde smon/ Rnam dag bde chen zhing gi smon lam mkhas grub rā ga a syas mdzad pa*. Boudanath, Nepal: Nyag rong lha rje rgyal sras 'jam dbyangs bstan 'dzin, 1932. BDRC W3CN1604

Situ Tenpai Nyinjé (Si tu Bstan pa'i nyin byed). *Oral Transmission of the Supreme Siddhas: A Commentary on the Prayer of the Definitive Mahāmudrā. Nges don phyag rgya chen po'i smon lam gyi 'grel pa grub mchog gi zhal lung.* In *Collected Works of Chökyi Jungné* (*Gsung 'bum* of Chos kyi 'byung gnas), vol. 8. Sansal, Kangra Dist., HP: Palpung sungrab nyamso khang: 1990. BDRC W26630.

Translator's Bibliography

Brunnhölzl, Karl. *The Center of the Sunlit Sky: Madhyamaka in the Kagyü Tradition.* Nitartha Institute Series. Ithaca, NY: Snow Lion, 2007.

Callahan, Elizabeth M., trans. *Moonbeams of Mahāmudrā,* by Dakpo Tashi Namgyal; With *Dispelling the Darkness of Ignorance* by Wangchuk Dorje, the Ninth Karmapa. The Tsadra Foundation Series. Boulder, CO: Snow Lion, 2019.

Dalton, Jacob P. "*Mahāmudrā* and *Samayamudrā* in the Dunhuang Documents and Beyond." In Jackson and Mathes, *Mahāmudrā in India and Tibet*, 123–41.

Dorje, Lama Sherab, trans. *The Eighth Situpa on the Third Karmapa's Mahamudra Prayer.* Boulder, CO: Snow Lion, 1995 and 2004.

Gray, David B. "Imprints of the 'Great Seal': On the expanding semantic range of the term *mudrā* in eighth through eleventh century Indian Buddhist literature." *JIABS* 34, nos. 1–2 (2011): 421–81.

Harding, Sarah. "As for the Blessing of Vajravārāhī, Marpa Lhodrakpa does not have it." Unpublished, Tsadra Foundation Blog, March 25, 2011.

Jackson, Roger R. *Tantric Treasures: Three Collections of Mystical Verse from Buddhist India*. Oxford: Oxford University Press, 2004.

Jackson, Roger R., and Klaus-Dieter Mathes, eds. *Mahāmudrā in India and Tibet*. Brill's Tibetan Studies Library 44. Leiden: Brill, 2019.

Jamgön Kongtrul Lodrö Tayé. *The Treasury of Knowledge, Book 6, Parts 1 and 2: Indo-Tibetan Classical Learning and Buddhist Phenomenology*. Translated by the Kalu Rinpoché Translation Group (Gyurme Dorje). Boston: Snow Lion, 2012.

———. *The Treasury of Knowledge, Book 6, Part 3: Frameworks of Buddhist Philosophy*. Translated by the Kalu Rinpoché Translation Group (Elizabeth M. Callahan). Ithaca, NY: Snow Lion, 2007.

———. *The Treasury of Knowledge, Book 8, Part 4: Esoteric Instructions*. Translated by the Kalu Rinpoché Translation Group (Sarah Harding). Ithaca, NY: Snow Lion, 2007.

———, comp. *The Treasury of Precious Instructions: Essential Teachings of the Eight Practice Lineages of Tibet, Volume 13: Zhije*. Translated by Sarah Harding. Boulder, CO: Snow Lion, 2019.

Mathes, Klaus-Dieter. "Blending the Sūtras with the Tantras: The Influence of Maitrīpa and His Circle on the Formation of *Sūtra Mahāmudrā* in the Kagyu Schools." In *Tibetan Buddhist Literature and Praxis: Studies in Its Formative Period, 900–1400: Proceedings of the Tenth Seminar of the International Association for Tibetan Studies*, edited by Ronald M. Davidson and Christian K. Wedemeyer, 201–27. Leiden: Brill, 2006.

———. "Can Sūtra Mahāmudrā be Justified on the Basis of Maitrīpa's Apratiṣṭhānavāda?" In *Pramāṇakīrtiḥ: Papers Dedicated to Ernst Steinkellner on the Occasion of His 70th Birthday*, edited by B. Kellner, H. Lasic, M. T. Much, H. Tauscher, 545–66. Wiener Studien zur Tibetologie und Buddhismuskunde 70, no. 2. Vienna: Arbeitskreis für tibetische und buddhistische Studien, 2007.

Nagarjuna's Letter to a Friend: With Commentary by Kangyur Rinpoche. Translated by the Padmakara Translation Group. Ithaca, NY: Snow Lion, 2005.

Tai Situ Rinpoche, XII Khentin. *The Third Karmapa's Mahāmudrā Prayer*. Translated by Rosemarie Fuchs. Ithaca, NY: Snow Lion, 2002.

Rhoton, Jared Douglas. *A Clear Differentiation of the Three Codes: Essential Distinctions among the Individual Liberation, Great Vehicle, and Tantric Systems*. Albany: State University of New York Press, 2002.

Rangjung Dorje, the Third Karmapa. *The Profound Inner Principles* with Jamgön Kongtrul Lodrö Taye's Commentary, *"Illuminating 'The Profound Principles.'"* Translated by Elizabeth M. Callahan. Boston: Snow Lion, 2014.

Roberts, Peter Alan, trans. *Mahāmudrā and Related Instructions: Core Teachings of the Kagyü Schools.* Boston: Wisdom Publications, 2011.

———. *The Mind of Mahāmudrā.* Boston: Wisdom Publications, 2014.

Situ Tenpai Nyinjé. "Oral Transmission of the Supreme Siddhas: A Commentary on Prayer for the Definitive Meaning, the Mahāmudrā." In Roberts, *Mahāmudrā and Related Instructions*, 175–288.

Index

A

Abhidharma, 63
abiding nature, 16, 53, 55, 57, 83, 93
  of ground, 35, 37
  meaning of, 67, 79
  of mind, 18, 69
  See also suchness
acceptance, 19, 77
action seal (*karmamudrā*), 3
Adornment of the Sūtras, 89
afflicted mentality, 41, 47
afflictions, 31, 51, 71, 73, 81
  freedom from, 89
  three, 27, 47
  See also individual afflictions
agitation, 61, 65
Akaniṣṭha, 85
all-base consciousness, 41, 47, 55, 105n23
analysis, 57. *See also under* meditation
"ancient school" (*snying ma*). *See* Nyingma lineage
appearances
  dualistic, 41
  and emptiness, 55
  as mind, 18, 45, 47, 57, 69, 91, 110n59
Arāga, 73
Aspiration Prayer for the Realm of Bliss, 91
Aspiration Prayer of Definitive Mahāmudrā (Rangjung Dorjé), 9, 15–20
aspirations
  accomplishing, 15, 19, 25
  for excellent support for path, 27, 29, 31
  for undeluded path, 35, 37
  for unmistaken practice, 39, 41, 43
  for wisdom that produces realization, 31, 33, 35
Atiśa, 5
attachment, 19, 65, 73, 77. *See also* fixation
attraction, 47, 59
aversion, 47, 59
awakening, 29, 31, 37, 81, 83. *See also* enlightenment
awareness, 91, 107n37
  timeless, 35, 41, 51, 61, 71
  See also four timeless awarenesses; innate awareness (*rang rig*); yoga of lucid awareness

B

bhusuku conduct, 83, 109n49
birth, 18, 57, 77, 87

blessings
of guru, 85
of hearing, 97
lineage guru's, 99
bliss, 4, 75, 91
of concentration, 81
penultimate, 35
See also great bliss
bodhicitta, relative, 35
Bodhisattva Commentaries, 93
bodhisattvas, 53, 79, 89
eyes of, 85
Bokar Rinpoché, 10
Buddha, 95. *See also* Śākyamuni Buddha
buddha eye, 87
buddha fields, 19, 85
buddha nature (Skt: *tathāgatagarbha*), 38, 105n25
buddha qualities, 19, 89, 91
accomplishing, 85
Buddha Word, three kinds, 33
buddhahood, 17, 55
buddhas, 19, 57, 79, 85, 87, 110n58
compassion of, 95
Buddha's thought, 93

C

Cakrasaṃvara, 11
calm abiding, 7, 18, 63, 65, 73
and higher insight, unification of, 91
nine techniques of, 107n38
See also nine methods of mental abiding
cause and effect, 37. *See also* karma
cessation, 18, 57, 77, 87
"chakgya chenpo" (*phyag rgya chen po*), 2. *See also* mahāmudrā
channels, 35
Chöd, 108
Chökyi Drakpa, fourth Shamar, 104n11
Chöwang Tulku Rinpoché, 12
clairvoyance, 19, 85. *See also* six clairvoyances
clarity-emptiness, 16
Clear Differentiation of the Three Codes (Kunga Gyaltsen), 7
compassion, 6, 10, 19, 20, 79, 81, 95
and emptiness, unity of, 83, 91
Concise Words on Mahāmudrā, 91
conduct, 17, 43, 83
yogic, 109
See also bhusuku conduct; yogic conduct
confidence, 16, 17, 18, 71
in Dharma, 97
in view, 43
connate union, 108n41
consciousness, 45, 47. *See also* eight consciousnesses
constituent (*khams*; Skt. *dhātu*), 105n25
contemplation, 33, 67
cyclic existence, 47, 57. *See also* samsara

D

Dakpo Kagyü. *See* Kagyü school
Dampa Sangyé (Kamalaśrī/Kamālaśīla), 107n39
death, 87
dedication of virtue, 25, 27
deities, 4, 15. *See also* gods; yidams
delusion, 18, 19, 57
incidental, 39
See also ignorance

demons, 73, 108n40
denial, extreme of, 16, 37, 67, 71
developed affinity (*rgyas 'gyur gyi rigs*), 35
devotion, 27, 83, 85, 99
Dharma, 31, 37, 59, 71, 97
dharma eye, 87
dharma seal (*dharmamudrā*), 3
Dharma talks, 1
dharmakāya, 16, 27, 37, 71, 73, 79
discriminating analysis. *See* analysis
distinct seeing (*lhag ger mthong*; Skt. *vipaśyanā*), 67. *See also* higher insight
distraction, 16, 43, 77
divine eye, 85, 87
dohās, 5, 103n6
doubt, 16, 65
  severing, 18, 33, 67
Drongmé tribe ('Brong smad), 11
dualistic extremes, 37
dualistic perception, 45, 47, 69
duality, 57, 91. *See also* dualistic extremes
dullness, 18, 61, 63, 65
Dunhuang manuscripts, 4
Düsum Khyenpa, 8–9

E

eight consciousnesses, purification of, 41. *See also* afflicted mentality; all-base consciousness; five sense consciousnesses; mental consciousness
eight remedies (*'du byed brgyad*), 65, 107n37
eight worldly concerns, 12, 59, 99
empowerment, 4, 7, 12
emptiness, 51, 57, 75, 81
  and clarity, unity of, 39, 61
  and compassion, unity of, 81, 83, 91
  and interdependence, unity of, 37, 43, 45, 53, 55
  and love, unity of, 77, 79, 81
  of mind, 43, 69
  of self, 47
enlightened activities, 91
enlightenment, 97. *See also* awakening
equal taste, 69, 75
equanimity, 105n27, 107n37
equipoise. *See* meditative equipoise
esoteric instructions, 4, 16, 33, 61, 63, 67, 69, 75, 79, 95. *See also* upadeśa
eternalism, 16, 37, 71
Exalted Child of the Victor. *See* bodhisattvas
examples
  chicken and egg, 45
  food, 89
  lotus, 81
  ocean, 27
  plantain tree, 99
  rabbit's horns, 8
  River Ganges, 99
existence, 17, 57, 59, 97, 99
  extreme of, 16, 37, 49, 51, 81, 83
  See also cyclic existence; samsara
eye of Dharma, 93

F

faith, 16, 27, 97, 107n37
  three kinds of, 29, 97, 99
Fifty Verses of Guru Devotion, 31
five eyes, 85, 87
five obscurations, 65

five sense consciousnesses, 41
five treatises of Maitreya, 109–110n53
fixation, 75, 77
  on dualistic elaborations, 91
  See also attachment
Fortunate Eon Sutra, 110n58
four great kings, 85
Four Hundred Verse Treatise (Āryadeva), 110n60
four kāyas, 10, 15, 27, 29. *See also* dharmakāya
four kinds of nonabiding, 105n27
four liberations, 23
four modes. *See* six limits and four modes
four mudrās, 3–4
four timeless awarenesses, 41
four yogas, 7, 91, 93. *See also* twelve stages
four-fold tantric initiation, 5
freedom from elaborations, 7, 35, 51, 93
freedom from extremes, 71, 106n28. *See also* dualistic extremes; eternalism; nihilism
freedoms and endowments, 16, 29, 31
fulfillment, 19, 85
fundamental transformation (*gnas gyur*), 41

G

Gampopa Sönam Rinchen, 5, 6, 7, 53, 69, 79, 81, 95, 108n41
genuine reality, 17
gods, 85
Gorampa Sönam Sengé, 7, 8
gradual path (*lam rim*), 5, 6–7
great bliss, 19, 51, 73, 91
great seal (*mahāmudrā*), 3, 4. *See also* mahāmudrā
ground. *See* abiding nature; two truths
guru offering, 99
guru practice, 99
gurus, 15, 29, 31, 37, 59, 67, 69, 75, 101
  authentic, 33
  blessings of, 85

H

happiness, 15, 29, 65, 67
heat, 6, 75
higher insight, 7, 65, 67, 69, 73
  and calm abiding, unification of, 91
  See also distinct seeing
highest yoga tantra, 4, 33
hindrances, 107n36. *See also* obstacles

I

ignorance, 45, 47, 67. *See also* delusion
Incessant Hell, 81
incidental stains, 12, 16, 18, 39, 41, 45, 47, 49, 57, 63. *See also* purification (*dag pa*)
Indian literature, 2
Indian mahāsiddhas, 5, 8
initiation, tantric. *See* four-fold tantric initiation
innate awareness (*rang rig*), 17, 47
innate body (*gnyug ma'i lus*), 35
intellect, 17, 19, 53, 75, 89
interdependence
  from emptiness, 37

and emptiness, unity of, 37, 43, 45, 53, 55
See also twelve links of interdependence
interdependent origination. *See* interdependence

J
Jamgön Kongtrul, 6, 7
Jamyang Palden. *See* Tsampa Rinpoché
jñānakāya, 41

K
Kadampa lineage, 5, 6
Kagyü school, 1, 2, 7, 39, 61, 83, 95
four early and eight later lineages, 5
lineage of, 4–6, 23
Kālacakra Tantra, 101
Kamtsang Kagyü. *See* Karma Kagyü lineage
karma, 27, 47. *See also* cause and effect
Karma Chönyi, 13
Karma Kagyü lineage, 9
Karma Ngedön Chökyi Lodrö. *See* Bokar Rinpoché
Karma Ngedön Tengyé Mawai Sengé Palzangpo. *See* Tsampa Rinpoché
Karma Pakshi, second Karmapa, 9
Karma Rinchen Dargyé, 1–2
kāyas, 91
Khakhyab Dorjé, fifteenth Karmapa, 12
Khenchen Lungrik Gyaltsen, 13
Khyabjé Kalu Rinpoché, 10
Kunzang Drolma, 13
Kunzik Situ Tenpai Nyinjé, 101

L
lam rim. *See* gradual path (*lam rim*)
Lama Tenpa, 103n3, 105n23
Lamp for the Minds of the Faithful (Bokar Rinpoché), 10
Letter to a Friend (Nāgārjuna), 65
Lhasa government, 11–12
liberation, 104n18
from fixation, 91
from not knowing, 33
logic, 33, 105n27
love, 19, 27
and emptiness, unity of, 77, 79, 81
lucid clarity, 18, 19, 45, 69, 75, 91, 93
and emptiness, unity of, 39, 91
ten signs of, 108–9n44
See also clarity-emptiness; vajra mind; yoga of lucid awareness

M
Machik Lapdrön, 108n40
madhyamaka, 18, 71, 105n27
definitive, 97
in tantras, 3–4
mahā, meaning of term, 2, 3
mahāmadhyamaka. *See* madhyamaka
mahāmudrā, 18, 43, 71, 85
compositions on, 1
controversy, 7–8
devotional, 23
etymology of, 2–3
Kagyü treatment of, 5–9
pristine awareness of, 7
timeless awareness of, 61

vajra yoga of, 16, 39
See also "chakgya chenpo" (*phyag rgya chen po*); great seal (*mahāmudrā*)
Mahāmudrā (practice), 23
Mahāmudrā Aspiration Prayer, 1
commentaries on, 1–2
mahāsandhi, 18, 71
mahāsukha svabhāvakāya, 27, 41
Mahāyāna Highest Continuum, 49
Maitreya Buddha, 110n58
Maitreyanātha, 61, 63
Maitrīpa, 5
malice, 65
Mañjuśrī, 53
Mantra Vehicle, 6, 12, 75. *See also* Vajrayāna
Mantrayāna. *See* Mantra Vehicle
Marpa Chökyi Lodrö, 4–5
Mathes, Klaus-Dieter, 8
maturation, 19, 85
meditation, 16, 17, 18, 19, 33, 41, 43, 57, 83, 93
analytic, 69
on emptiness, 79
head, foot, and body of, 83
strength of, 87
taking into experience through, 59, 61, 63
See also calm abiding; higher insight; meditative equipoise; meditative stability
meditative equipoise, 43, 77, 89, 93
meditative stability, 63, 65. *See also* five obscurations
Mendong Tsampa Rinpoché, 1, 9–14
mental consciousness, 41
mental continuum, 57
mental nonengagement (*yid la mi byed pa*), 5
middle way, 17, 51, 71
Mikyö Dorjé, eighth Karmapa, 97
Milarepa, 5, 6, 81
mind
abiding nature of, 69
afflicted by three poisons, 27
and appearances, 45, 47
appearances as, 18
displays of, 17
emptiness of, 43, 69
empty essence of, 17, 18
imperceptible, 18, 67
innate, 35, 77
nature of, 4
nonexistence of, 49
phenomena as, 43
true nature of, 17
mindfulness, 107n37
Moonbeams of Mahāmudrā (Tashi Namgyal), 5–6
mudrā, meaning of term, 2, 3, 4. *See also* four mudrās; "seal" (*mudrā; phyag rgya*)

N

Nāgārjuna, 39, 49, 51, 55, 79, 81, 97, 106n35. *See also Letter to a Friend* (Nāgārjuna)
Nāropa, 5, 8, 91. *See also* Six Dharmas of Nāropa
nectar, 31, 93
"new school" (*gsar ma*), 4
nihilism, 16, 37, 67, 71, 106n28
nine methods of mental abiding, 65
nirmāṇakāya, 27

nirvana, 49, 57, 83
phenomena of, 37
and samsara, basis of, 17
nonexistence, 37, 49, 51
nondistraction, 16, 43, 83
nonduality, 53, 77. *See also* equal taste
nonmeditation, 7, 93
nonreferential, 107n35
nonrejection, 77
nonself, 87
nonthought, 19, 75, 91
nonvirtue, 81
Nyingma lineage, 4, 9

O

obscurations, 19, 91, 93. *See also* five obscurations; hindrances
obstacles, 31. *See also* hindrances; obscurations
one taste, 7, 91, 93
one-pointedness, 7, 107n38
Oral Transmission of the Supreme Siddhas, The (Tenpai Nyinjé), 1, 3
ordinary individuals, 13, 27. *See also* sentient beings
ordinary mind, 19, 77
Ornament of Dakpo Kagyü Thought (Mendong Tsampa), 1

P

pacification, 73
Pacification of Suffering (Zhijé), 107n39
Padma Karpo, 8
Pakmo Drupa, 71, 73
path of accumulation, 93
path of application, 93
path of seeing, 93
peace, extreme of, 37, 83
"People's Dohā, The" (Saraha), 59, 106n33
Perfection of Wisdom, 73
perfection of wisdom (*prajñāpāramitā*), 6
Perfections Vehicle, 7, 93
permanence, 77, 106n28
phenomena
and mind, 73
as mind, 43
perfection of, 87
pledge seal (*samayamudrā*), 3, 4
prayer, 1, 25, 95, 109n52, 110n54. *See also individual prayers*
Prayer of Excellent Conduct, 109n52
Prayer of Samantabhadra's Conduct, 89
preliminaries, 59
pure realms, 89
pure thoughts, 27
purification (*dag pa*), 41, 49, 89. *See also* twofold purity (*dag pa gnyis ldan*)

R

Rangjung Dorjé, third Karmapa, 1, 9–10, 23, 97
Rechungpa, 5, 8
refinement, 85
result of, 19, 39, 41
relative truth, 37
revulsion, 83
rūpakāya, 37. *See also* buddha qualities

S

Sakya Paṇḍita Kunga Gyaltsen, 7
Śākyamuni Buddha, 101, 110n58
saṃbhogakāya, 27
samsara, 19, 49, 53, 55, 79
  and nirvana, basis of, 17
  phenomena of, 37
  See also cyclic existence
Saraha, 5, 57, 59, 61, 95
Śavaripa, 5
scripture, 33
"seal" (*mudrā; phyag rgya*), 3
Secret Mantra Vehicle, 12
self, as external object, 45, 47. *See also* nonself
self-cherishing, 81
sentient beings, 15, 19, 27, 57, 79, 87, 95, 106n32
  maturing, 85, 89
  See also ordinary individuals
seven jewels, 99
Severance/Chö (*gcod*) lineage, 9
Shangpa lineage, 10
Siṁha Buddha, 110n58
single flavor. *See* one taste
single-pointed yoga, 93
Situ Paṇchen Chökyi Jungné, Tenpai Nyinjé, 1, 3, 59
six clairvoyances, 85, 87, 89, 91, 93
Six Dharmas of Nāropa, 5, 6, 23
six limits and four modes, 33, 104–5n21
six-branch yoga, 93, 110n57
sixth lion emanation. *See* Rangjung Dorjé, third Karmapa
space, 19, 49, 77, 101
spiritual master. *See* gurus
spiritual partner/consort, 2, 4
spontaneous presence, 69
stages of the path, 91, 93
study, 16, 33
subsequent attainment, 93
suchness, 33, 77, 93, 97, 99
  realization of, 2
  synonyms for, 35
  See also abiding nature
suffering, 15, 19, 29, 79
Suhṛllekha (Nāgārjuna), 107n36
superimpositions, 57
  extreme of, 37
  severing, 43, 45, 67
supreme path, 37
sutra mahāmudra, 6–7, 8
sutras, 96, 98, 100
svabhāvakāya. *See* mahāsukha svabhāvakāya

T

tantras, 8, 9, 10, 12, 95, 99. *See also* highest yoga tantra
tantric instructions. *See* esoteric instructions
ten signs, 75
ten strengths, 87
thoughts, 15, 18, 63, 65, 67, 73, 77, 107n36
  as dharmakāya, 71, 110n59
  See also pure thoughts
three baskets (*Tripiṭaka*), 33
three doors, 59
three great Maitreya Dharmas, 91
Three Jewels, 29, 37
three kāyas, 41, 47, 49
three spheres, 15, 27
three times, 15, 61, 89
three wisdoms, 16, 33, 69
Tibetan Buddhism, 2. *See also individual lineages*

Tilopa, 5
true nature (*dharmatā*), 53
true reality, 19, 69, 79. *See also* ultimate reality
Tsampa Rinpoché, 11
Tsurphu Monastery, 12
twelve links of interdependence, 45
twelve stages (*sa;* Skt. *bhūmi*), 93
two accumulations, 16, 37
two kāyas, 35, 41
two truths, 16, 57. *See also* relative truth; ultimate truth
twofold knowledge (*mkhyen pa gnyis ldan*), 41
twofold purity (*dag pa gnyis ldan*), 41

U

ultimate path, 93
ultimate reality, 53, 57. *See also* true reality
ultimate state, 85, 87, 93
ultimate truth, 37
uncontrived innate state, 18, 61
union, 4, 105n27, 108n41
  of clarity-emptiness, 16
  of emptiness and compassion, 83, 91
upadeśa, 99. *See also* esoteric instructions

V

Vajra Court of the Bodhi Medicine Tree, 13
vajra mind, 45. *See also* lucid clarity
vajra of mind, 39
vajra scriptures, 95
Vajradhara, 23, 83, 99
Vajravārāhī, 5
Vajrayāna, 7. *See also* Mantra Vehicle
valid cognition, 33, 108n41
Vasubandhu, 87
victors. *See* buddhas
vigor, 16, 29, 31
Vinaya, 71
vipaśyanā. *See* distinct seeing (*lhag ger mthong*; Skt. *vipaśyanā*)
virtue, 15, 27, 29, 31, 55, 99, 107n36
vital drops, 35
vital winds, 35, 75

W

wind-mind, 12
wisdom, 16, 31, 93, 97, 99
  free of reference, 27
  from meditation, 33
  nonconceptual, 69
  See also three wisdoms
wisdom eye, 87
worldly activities. *See* eight worldly concerns; three doors

Y

yidams, 15. *See also* deities
yoga of inner heat, 6
yoga of lucid awareness, 6
yogic conduct, 109n49

About the Translator

Sarah Harding has been studying and practicing Buddhism since 1974, and has been teaching and translating since completing a three-year retreat in 1980 under the guidance of Kyabjé Kalu Rinpoché. She was a professor at Naropa University for twenty-five years, in Boulder, Colorado, where she currently resides, and has been a fellow of the Tsadra Foundation since 2000. She specializes in literature with a focus on tantric practice. Her publications include *Creation and Completion: Essential Points of Tantric Meditation*; *The Treasury of Knowledge: Esoteric Instructions*; *Niguma, Lady of Illusion*; and four volumes on Chöd, Zhijé, and Shangpa Kagyü from the *Treasury of Precious Instructions*.

What to Read Next from Wisdom Publications

Creation and Completion
Essential Points of Tantric Meditation
Jamgön Kongtrul
Translated by Sarah Harding

"Creation and completion meditation is the cornerstone of tantric Buddhist practice, and draws upon a rich array of techniques and presumptions relating to moral culitvation. This book will be of great interest to both scholars and practitioners of Tibetan Buddhism."—Janet Gyatso, Hershey Chair of Buddhist Studies, Harvard University

Four Tibetan Lineages
Core Teachings of Pacification, Severance, Shangpa Kagyü, and Bodongpa
Translated by Sarah Harding

Drawing primarily from the Pacification, Severance, Shangpa Kagyü, and Bodongpa traditions, *Four Tibetan Lineages* presents some of Tibet's most transformative yet lesser-known teachings on meditative practice.

Ornament of Precious Liberation
By Gampopa
Translated by Ken Holmes
Foreword by His Holiness the Karmapa

"This text has the power of a direct transmission from master to student . . . Though there are several earlier translations of *Ornament of Precious Liberation*, this translation is the most readable and faithful."—His Holiness the Karmapa, Ogyen Trinley Dorje

Mahāmudrā and Related Instructions
Core Teachings of the Kagyü Schools
Translated by Peter Alan Roberts

"This collection is a treasury of 'great seal' teachings from the most renowned gurus of the Mahāmudrā lineage, each text precious beyond compare. Every page exudes freshness of realization, holding the keys to our own personal awakening."—Judith Simmer-Brown, Naropa University, author of *Dakini's Warm Breath*

Sounds of Innate Freedom
The Indian Texts of Mahāmudrā
Translated and introduced by Karl Brunnhölzl

This collection offers a brilliant window into the richness of the vast ocean of Indian mahāmudrā texts cherished in all Tibetan lineages, particularly in the Kagyü tradition, giving us a clear view of the sources of one of the world's great contemplative traditions.

About Wisdom Publications

Wisdom Publications is the leading publisher of classic and contemporary Buddhist books and practical works on mindfulness. To learn more about us or to explore our other books, please visit our website at wisdomexperience.org or contact us at the address below.

Wisdom Publications
199 Elm Street
Somerville, MA 02144 USA

We are a 501(c)(3) organization, and donations in support of our mission are tax deductible.

Wisdom Publications is affiliated with the Foundation for the Preservation of the Mahayana Tradition (FPMT).